FLYING COLD

THE ADVENTURES OF RUSSEL MERRILL,
PIONEER ALASKAN AVIATOR

FLYING COLD

THE ADVENTURES OF RUSSEL MERRILL,
PIONEER ALASKAN AVIATOR

ROBERT MERRILL MACLEAN
AND
SEAN ROSSITER

Epicenter Press
Fairbanks/Seattle

Editor: Don Graydon
Proofreader: Christine Ummel
Design and typesetting: Newman Design/Illustration
Cover illustration: Byron Birdsall
Cover design: Leslie Newman
Printer: Network Graphics
Binder: Lincoln-Allen Bindery

Library of Congress Cataloging-in-Publication Data

MacLean, Robert Merrill, 1924 –

Flying cold: the adventures of Russel Merrill, pioneer Alaskan aviator/Robert Merrill MacLean and Sean Rossiter; foreword by Ted Spencer.

    p.   cm.

    Includes index.

ISBN 0-945397-32-1: $34.95 — ISBN 0-945397-33-X (pbk.): $24.95

    1. Merrill, Russel, 1894-1929. 2. Bush pilots—Alaska—Biography. 3. Air pilots—United States—Biography.

I. Rossiter, Sean, 1946 –   II. Title.

TL540.M3937M33 1994

629.13'092—dc20   94-27416

[B]   CIP

To order autographed copies of *FLYING COLD*, mail $34.95 for a hardcover edition (Washington residents add $2.87 state sales tax) or $24.95 for a softcover edition (Washington residents add $2.05 state sales tax) plus $5.00 for Priority-Mail shipping to: Epicenter Press, Box 82368, Kenmore Station, Seattle, WA 98028-0368.

Booksellers: Retail discounts are available from our trade distributor, Graphic Arts Center Publishing Co., Box 10306, Portland, OR 97210. Phone 800-452-3032.

PRINTED IN THE UNITED STATES OF AMERICA
First printing, September, 1994
10 9 8 7 6 5 4 3 2 1

PHOTO CREDITS

Anchorage Museum of History and Art
1, 4, 5, 6, 7, 33, 39, 56, 59, 101, 133, 158, 171, 172

Merrill Collection, Alaska Aviation Heritage Museum
i, ii, vi, viii, 8, 9, 10, 16, 18, 21, 24, 25, 29, 32, 37, 42, 44, 48, 49, 51, 62, 65, 67, 69, 71, 72, 74, 80, 84, 90, 92, 106, 107, 108, 109, 114, 115, 119, 121, 122, 123, 124, 127, 131, 135, 137, 142, 143, 145, 147, 153, 157, 160, 165, 170, 173, 174

Seward Museum—Alaska Aviation Heritage Museum
30, 34

Eddie Brown Collection/Stevens
167

Walter Brewington/Stevens
31

Gordon MacKenzie Collection/Stevens
94, 97

Katherine MacLean
178

Alan M. James
178

Gwen Jones/Stevens
168

Photograph page ii: Russel Merrill stands before the heavily damaged fuselage of *Anchorage No. 1* before he and Alonzo Cope repaired it at Lockanok in June and July of 1927. The fuselage was broken completely apart at the pilot's cockpit just to the right in this picture.

ACKNOWLEDGMENTS

A substantial portion of this book was derived from my mother's 1930 manuscript *Skyriders of Alaska*, by Thyra Merrill in collaboration with Elizabeth R. Jacobs. Incorporated are accounts by Alonzo Cope, Charles G. Clarke, and Gus Gelles, as noted in the text. Sir Hubert Wilkins graciously wrote a preface to that work, which is included herein.

Ted Spencer, founder of the Alaska Aviation Heritage Museum, has been a guiding influence, providing me with the historical significance of my father's accomplishments, unsurpassed knowledge of airplanes of the period, and his feel for the material that readers look for in Alaska aviation books.

I had no previous experience in writing, but fortunately many talented people contributed to this book. I want to thank the following for making it the fine product it is.

Sean Rossiter, for making a book out of my amateur manuscript and educating me on the art of writing.

Bob Stevens, the authoritative historian of Alaska aviation, for generously furnishing pictures and historical information, a careful review of the entire book, and his encouragement.

Diane Brenner of the Anchorage Museum of History and Art, for additional pictures and papers; Wanda Griffin, daughter of Gus Gelles, for her helpful research; Bruce Merrell of the Z. J. Loussac Public Library at Anchorage; Margaret Weatherly of Reeve Aleutian Airways; Ed Phillips, authority on Travel Air planes; and Epicenter Press, the publisher.

Finally I thank my loving wife, Marge, and our four great daughters, Janet, Joan, Ann, and Kathy, for their support and input.

Robert Merrill MacLean

CONTENTS

Opposite: Russel Merrill's *Anchorage No. 1* sits on the river bed at Wiseman on May 13, 1928, after a flight from Fairbanks. The weather was clear when this plane and Noel Wien's Stinson left later in the day for Barrow, but changed for the worse after they crossed the mountains.

It is a distinguished company, as a rule, that one sees on the boats sailing for Alaska. Men with thoughts and intellects far above the level indicated by their clothes and manners. Men who have communed with nature in her ruggedest form, who have faced hardship, toil, and even death with a steadfastness not necessarily acquired by city dwellers.

Occasionally among them there will be seen sturdy salesmen, not the wise-cracking, storytelling type met on the extra fare trains, but the type of man who has come in on the ground floor, worked his way through the various stages of his calling and then, because of his sheer goodwill toward men, has been selected to contact and canvass among men in the north who are quick to see and sift realities from the unreal.

But among the passengers travelling north with us in 1927 were a few of an entirely different type. They were the men of our Detroit News Expedition to the Arctic. Ben Eielson—clean-cut, wholesome, and attractive. Joe Crosson—boyish, frank, lovable, and cheerful. Orval Porter—quiet, unassuming, capable, dependable, and loyal. Arthur M. Smith—gray-haired, scholarly, a journalist with a winning smile and a generous degree of humor.

Among them I soon noticed another of their type. The stranger was Russel Merrill. He was easily placed among the class of men found in aviation: clear-eyed, earnest, capable, with positive and deliberate yet prompt action that signified ability as a pilot. He expressed a dogged determination and an intensity of purpose that is more than courage. It was not only the ability to fight against tremendous odds, when the odds were present and inevitable; it was the keen desire to surmount difficulties, the eagerness to do difficult, worthwhile things, that made Merrill conspicuous.

I had heard of his exploits in pioneering the route in southeastern Alaska and learned that he was to be in charge of the flying from Anchorage. He was just the type to inspire the admiration of the prospectors and trappers and the type also that

Opposite: Russel Merrill, fur mukluks on his feet, prepares to climb into the open cockpit of the Travel Air cabin plane on March 10, 1928. He was on his way from Anchorage to Lawing with a load of furs to intercept the train that would take the furs to Seward for shipment to auction in Seattle.

would fit in well with the big-game hunters and the government officials who would from time to time take advantage of the flying services in Alaska. He had proved his courage and his daring and his ability to fly, and there was no doubt about his sincere belief that flying in Alaska would be of tremendous advantage in the development of the country.

He was of the type that puts a purpose before personal pleasures and comforts. But we wondered—those of us who were at that time single—whether it was wise for a man who was so anxious to put his whole heart into his work, to be married and the father of two healthy and handsome boys. We soon found out that if married to the kind of a girl we found Thyra Merrill to be, that it would not only be possible to do pioneering work such as that upon which Russel Merrill had set his heart, but that with the help and the faith of such a woman it would be a joy and a pleasure.

There was no doubt about Merrill's ability to do the work of a pilot of airplanes. So long as the machine was in order, all would be well. But the Arctic is a hard mistress for those inexperienced in her ways, and I have often marvelled at the chances taken in Alaska by pilots who, without experience in foot travel over the dreary wastes, ventured forth in their frail machines carrying the minimum of supplies, chancing a forced landing and a possible walk to some point in civilization. Explorers often get credit for daring and courage, but no explorer that I know would dare to set out as did those pilots in Alaska, with little or no training in ground travel and few conveniences, supplies, or aides in case of accidents.

Take for instance the story as told by Mrs. Merrill of Russel Merrill's flight to Point Barrow with the Fox Film men: six of them setting out for a hazardous flight over uninhabited country with only a few days' food supply and no adequate provision for walking home. It is almost a miracle that their lives were saved.

Eielson and I pioneered that route and it has been crossed now a hundred times by planes, but nevertheless it would be foolhardy to set out on that flight without a month's supply of food or some provision to obtain it. Some of the chances taken by the fliers of Alaska are described in a matter-of-fact, straight-out way in this book, but they make the hairs of a seasoned explorer, even as I am, stand on end. The risks are not so obvious, perhaps, to those who do not know the country over which the men flew on their errands of service and mercy.

Mrs. Merrill has given us a fine outline of facts that cover the history of flying in Alaska. It is a job worthy and well done by one whose womanly courage is of the kind that made possible the great pioneering developments of history.

Sir Hubert Wilkins
Leader
Arctic Expeditions 1926, 1927, 1928

The years 1929 and 1930 were a tragic time for Alaska's aviators. The first woman pilot to fly in the North Country, Marvel Crosson, died in an August 1929 air race in the United States. In November of 1929, Alaska's most famous pioneer pilot, Ben Eielson, and his mechanic, Earl Borland, disappeared while flying a relief mission in Siberia. Ralph Wien, brother of famed pilot Noel Wien, died in October 1930 when the diesel-powered Bellanca Pacemaker he was piloting crashed at Kotzebue.

Another star fell from Alaskan skies during this period as well. Yet few people today know of this Alaskan aviation pioneer and hero. It is not that his accomplishments were lackluster or of little consequence. It wasn't that he was not lionized by the media, because his exploits appeared in the national press numerous times. He did die young after too brief a career. This factor may have a lot to do with his present obscurity. He also perished while pioneering in America's last frontier, known for its transient fortune-seeking immigrants. Alaska's population is notorious for its turnover. With each generation, the facts are diluted to myth and the myth fades a little more with each era. Such has been the fate of Russel Hyde Merrill.

Russ Merrill was a gangly young man, quiet and unpretentious. He shied away from the limelight; you could see this characteristic in photos of him. He had boyish enthusiasm for high adventure and apparently knew little fear. He flew primitive flying machines into hostile far-flung areas that could kill him should his airplane fail. And sadly, this was the story of his ending.

Russ Merrill was no harebrained wild man. From reading his letters to his family and professional associates, Merrill is revealed as an intellectual explorer interested in mapping topography for the U.S. Geological Survey. Flying over uncharted mountain ranges, large bodies of water, and vast expanses of tundra, he was the space astronaut of his day. He pioneered the use of the airplane to facilitate wilderness tourism in Alaska. He brought aviation to Anchorage the same year Lindbergh flew the Atlantic.

Merrill has all but been forgotten by the Alaskan public, as have many of the twentieth-century pioneers. He represents a small cadre of extraordinary people who exhibited courage, resourcefulness, ingenuity, and tenacity, tempered with humor and a true love for their fellow human beings.

Merrill died doing his job, flying support for yet another Alaskan enterprise. He left behind his little family, friends, and compatriots to mourn and wonder as to his fate. He also left a legacy that was the model for the twentieth-century Alaskan pioneer. Today we would do well to reflect on this man's contributions and accomplishments. He set a standard of performance in which we can all find inspiration as we rocket into the twenty-first century.

Ted Spencer
Executive Director
Alaska Aviation Heritage Museum
Anchorage

My first memory is from 1928, in Anchorage, Alaska. I am flying upside down, looking at the houses below from the open cockpit of a biplane. Anchorage looks like a toy city above my head. Although I am only four years old, I have no fear. Looking back at the rear cockpit, I see my father with a smile on his face and feel the exhilaration he radiates.

All my recollections of my father are happy ones because he was full of life. He thrived on challenges; to him they were unfolding adventures.

After my dad was lost, I refused to believe he was dead. I couldn't understand why God would allow a good person to be killed when his family and others needed him. I finally came to realize that even when a life is cut short, good can come from it. Russel Merrill's life is a sterling example.

My mother, the consummate Russel Merrill booster, threw herself into writing a book on his life. They had been very close, and getting busy writing about their life in Alaska was Thyra Merrill's way of dealing with her loss. With the help of Alonzo Cope, Russel's mechanic and companion, and Grace Clarke, Anchorage Air Transport's secretary, my mother collected all the records she could find about my father's flights: three hundred letters, two hundred photos, fifty pieces of technical literature, a hundred newspaper clippings, three maps, and many journal accounts.

She completed her manuscript, titled *Skyriders of Alaska.* Sir Hubert Wilkins, the Arctic and Antarctic explorer, wrote a foreword (published in this book on page ix). But she couldn't find a publisher in the Depression years. We then moved to California, where she earned one of the first commercial pilot's licenses held by a woman, and in 1934 she remarried. A busy life followed, and the manuscript was set aside.

I inherited the manuscript and my dad's papers in 1989 after both my mother and stepfather died. I had barely gotten to work on this present book when Ted Spencer, executive director of the Alaska Aviation Heritage Museum in Anchorage, tracked me down. He told me of the gap in Alaska aviation history caused by the lack of firsthand information on Russel Merrill, the most prominent flier in the Anchorage area before 1930. Ted Spencer's push moved my book project into gear.

Fortunately, Sean Rossiter—author of the beautiful book *Legends of the Air*, about airplanes in Seattle's Museum of Flight—agreed to be the writer on the project. In addition to the original papers and pictures and my mother's manuscript, we used many other sources as we worked on the book. Among these were the Alaska Aviation Heritage Museum, Anchorage Museum of History and Art, Z. J. Loussac Public Library at Anchorage, newspaper articles, and Robert W. Stevens' authoritative two-volume *Alaskan Aviation History 1897–1930* (Polynyas Press, Des Moines, Washington, 1990).

This resulting book is full of firsthand accounts that take the reader back seven decades into the first days of flying in Alaska. An abundance of photographs, many never before published, flesh out the narrative. The story told in this book is not artificially dramatized or enhanced—not that the tale wants for adventure. It's an honest glimpse into history that is more exhilarating than any fiction.

This is the true story of a great man who risked everything to follow his dreams, faced challenges that have no parallel in our modern world, and ultimately gave his life to help open the way for air travel in Alaska. This is the story of my father.

Robert Merrill MacLean
Seattle, Washington
February 20, 1994

> I WAS ALONE, SUSPENDED BY NOTHING BUT
> AIR. IT CERTAINLY IS A FUNNY FEELING TO
> KNOW THAT YOUR DESTINY RESTS COMPLETELY
> WITH YOUR OWN KNOWLEDGE OF THE GAME.
>
> — RUSSEL MERRILL,
>   IN A LETTER DESCRIBING HIS
>   FIRST SOLO FLIGHT

CHAPTER ONE
THE TAKEOFF

"CONTACT!"

RUSSEL MERRILL'S VOICE FROM THE COCKPIT CAME CLEARLY TO THYRA MERRILL AS SHE STOOD ON THE BANK OF THE WILLAMETTE RIVER NEAR PORTLAND, OREGON. SHADING HER EYES FROM THE NOONDAY SUN, SHE WATCHED CYRIL KRUGNER, THE LITTLE MECHANIC, BALANCE HIMSELF ON THE HULL OF THE FLYING BOAT, READY TO TURN OVER THE PROPELLER. ROY DAVIS, MERRILL'S PARTNER AND OWNER OF THE WAR-SURPLUS CURTISS F-BOAT, WAS WAVING FAREWELL FROM HIS PLACE IN THE COCKPIT.

"Con..."

The motor caught, loosing a roar that swallowed the last syllable of Krugner's reply that morning of May 17, 1925. With the explosion of sound on the peaceful air, Thyra felt a corresponding quickening of her pulse. The men were off—off to Alaska!

Now Krugner was back in his place in the cockpit and waving, too. Merrill, busy at the controls, did not turn his head. But in a moment he "wiggled the flippers" (ailerons suspended on wires between the wings), and Thyra knew he was saying goodbye. The airplane taxied out.

Russel had put much of himself into this flight, starting with assembling the Curtiss Model F flying boat on the Willamette with his own hands, which took most of April. The aircraft had to be tuned like a grand piano: wires, tensioned by turnbuckles, furnished much of its structural strength and operated its flight surfaces.

The original Curtiss 100-horsepower OXX-3 V8 motor had been replaced by an overhauled K-6 inline six-cylinder engine that, on paper at least, of-

Overleaf: Russel Merrill stands on the bank of the Willamette River near Portland, Oregon, in front of the Curtiss Model F flying boat that he, Roy Davis, and Cyril Krugner flew to Alaska in 1925. The trip was only the second nonmilitary flight ever completed up the Pacific Coast to Alaska.

fered 50 more horsepower. The rebuilt motor caused continual hassles, such as clogged gasoline strainers. Merrill finally had the plane airworthy after test-flying the F-boat for more than two weeks, ironing out each wrinkle as it appeared.

The airplane looked like a speedboat with wings until it caught a breeze that morning and lifted off the water. The motor and large propeller loomed behind the three men in the wide single seat as the rest of the plane began to blend with the sky. Thyra would later write, in the unpublished manuscript she titled *Skyriders of Alaska:*

I stood, rooted, until it was small and high overhead, until it vanished, heading, like the birds, northward. Then I turned and went slowly back to the car where the children waited with their nurse. Bobby, the baby, lay in Millie's lap, and Dick played contentedly on the seat.

"Well, Mrs. Merrill, I see they got off." There was that note of forced cheerfulness in the girl's voice that one uses in times of grave danger. I laughed and started the car.

"Yes, Millie, and we're left behind. But I'll have a wire from Mr. Merrill in a few days and then we'll be off, too, to meet him."

"Oh, Mrs. Merrill, do you think so? That airplane looked awful clumsy to me. I wouldn't go up for a million dollars. It must be a terrible long way to Alaska."

"Nearly a thousand miles, Millie."

"Well, all I can say is, it looked kind of clumsy to me." She hugged the baby closer and looked at him. "Poor little mite," she added darkly.

Turning into our own drive, I tried to distract her from premonitions of trouble.

RUSSEL MERRILL'S FAMILY BASE OF ACHIEVERS AND STRONG TIES GAVE HIM THE EMOTIONAL STRENGTH AND SELF-CONFIDENCE TO OVERCOME THE TOUGHEST OBSTACLES.

Russel Merrill grew up
in Des Moines, Iowa.

*"Don't you want to go to Alaska with me? It will be a fine
trip on the boat, and you'll see a lot of interesting things."*

*"Oh, yes, I want to go, Mrs. Merrill." She looked towards the
house surrounded by lawn and the rich color of massed flowers
warmed by the May sun.*

*"But I can't see why you want to leave such a nice place and
all. Alaska's going to be an awful place to take babies to."*

*"Of course not. Ketchikan is almost as large as your home-
town. We'll have a house or live at a hotel. I don't know much
about the country myself, but it certainly isn't as primitive as
you seem to think."*

*"Well, I don't know..." She was still shaking her head as she
trundled the babies off to their naps.*

*Undoubtedly it was mystifying to our friends that Russel
was giving up a promising business career as an official in a
manufacturing concern and starting out in a frail airplane for an
unknown country to barnstorm. I knew they must be thinking,
"Wild goose chase!" They couldn't understand his consuming
interest in aviation nor see his vision of starting an aviation service in Alaska.*

Millie's instincts were sound. The first leg of Russel Merrill's epic thou-
sand-mile flight to Alaska, only the second nonmilitary flight up the Pacific
Coast, lasted all of about eight minutes. An oil leak had them back on the
Willamette. Krugner corrected it in fifteen minutes.

Then for two-and-a-half hours they taxied up and down the river, rock-
ing the plane and shifting their weight back and forth, but they were unable

to get into the air. The plane was overloaded with three passengers and sixty pounds of gear. With much of the weight in the bow locker and no wind, they needed help getting off the water. Finally the waves of a passing steamer gave them the boost they needed to lift off. This time they had better luck and were really on their way, heading first to Seattle.

Russel Hyde Merrill was born April 8, 1894, in Des Moines, Iowa. The Merrills were well-to-do and socially prominent. The family owned a number of farms, as well as properties in Des Moines. Russel's great-uncle was governor of Iowa from 1868 to 1872. Russel and his brothers, Jerry and Edward, were very close, supported each other, and stayed in touch all their lives. This family base of achievers and strong ties gave Russel the emotional strength and self-confidence to overcome the toughest obstacles.

Russel Merrill's family poses on the porch of their home in Des Moines, Iowa, on January 12, 1913. From left: father Samuel; Russel (age 18); mother Fannie; brothers Edward and Jerry.

Young Russel was an all-around student and athlete at West Des Moines High School. He placed second in the high jump at a regional track meet during his senior year, was a member of the school's social club, and played the flute in the school band. He attended Grinnell College, Iowa, for three years, and then transferred to Cornell University.

The onset of World War I led him to give up his studies in chemical engineering six months before graduation in order to enlist in the Navy on

Russel Merrill (right) and his brothers, Jerry (left) and Edward, are pictured at Palo Alto, California, in 1922 at the time of their mother's death.

May 11, 1917. Merrill patrolled the Atlantic coast for enemy craft in a boat donated by the father of a friend, but he soon felt the need for duty that was more active and interesting.

Transferred to the Naval Aviation Service, he graduated among the top eight students from ground school at the Massachusetts Institute of Technology and was sent to Key West, Florida, for flight training. There he received his first instruction in Curtiss N9 seaplanes—float-equipped versions of the Army's famous JN-4D Jenny—which cruised at 65 miles per hour.

Navy flight training was rigorous because much of the flying was done over water, with its penalties for imperfect navigation and dangers from fog and storm. Key West offered only five planes for fifty prospective pilots, so those not qualified to fly solo often got only ten to forty minutes of actual flying a day. The rest of the time they helped move the planes or worked on the engines. Merrill wrote home:

If you have ever enjoyed a scenic railway, you will be crazy about flying. We always expect the unexpected and are never disappointed.

Our plane has been the original hard-luck machine the past week. My last hop was nearly a week ago. We have put in three new motors in the meantime; the last was from the factory and couldn't find an excuse for not working. Today I was a bit rusty and broke a pontoon on landing. However, my instructor suffered under the delusion that I could fly. So he put the squadron commander in the front seat and told me to show him how good I was.

I took him off the water in fine style and made some turns at which he clapped his hands. But he shut off the engine while we were going with the wind. Of course, I nosed the machine down, spiralled down, and happened to find myself with the plane intact on the water heading into the wind. However, orders today were that all turns were to be to the left—and my spiral was to the right! Also my landing was nothing to rave about. But he raved about both spiral and landing, as much as he ever does, and told me to land a few more times.

The next time I misjudged the height about three feet and made a very poor landing. The next happened to be pretty fair, and bringing him back to the station I made a creditable one.

After this exhibition, he told me I could solo! Consequently I taxied out a little way, then cut back on the motor to drift a minute and wipe off my goggles. Alas, the motor died! I tried frantically to start it, but the motor boat had to come out and throw me a line to keep me from drifting ashore. A machinist's mate on the motor boat cranked the plane for me, and finally I got off.

Then came thirteen minutes of the best little thrills invented. All this means that I was alone, suspended by nothing but air. It certainly is a funny feeling to know that your destiny rests completely with your own knowledge of the game.

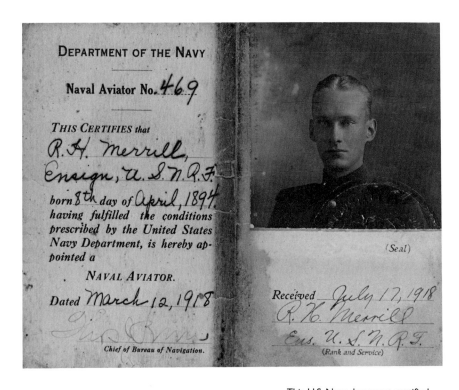

This U.S. Navy document certified Russel Merrill's appointment as a naval aviator on March 12, 1918, while he was stationed at Key West, Florida. He was the 469th person to earn the gold wings of a naval aviator.

Russel Merrill stands before a Curtiss R-6L twin-pontoon seaplane, one of the types of planes he flew at Cape May, New Jersey, in 1918. Merrill was chief pilot at Cape May Naval Station.

During the following month, Merrill progressed to the point where he was permitted to do aerobatics. He showed he had all the right instincts.

Yesterday I had my first stunt hop. I had done a couple of stalls but hadn't been in any loops or spins. I don't think the squadron commander knew this, as he let me go up alone. Of course everyone wants to do this, but few get away with it. Permission to loop is also much sought after and is quite rare, as looping is apt to strain the machine, especially water-machines. I was glad that I was at Key West; Miami is the only other station where they allow stunts, and that station is for advanced flying.

With great glee I climbed up to 6,700 feet, in order to have room for some fun. You see, we must come out of all stunts above 2,000 feet. First I looped, making a rather poor one. What a funny sensation when I was on my back at the top of the loop! The strap across my lap was all that held me, of course; the belt was a little loose, which added to the sensation. Next on the program was a tail spin, so I nosed the machine up a little on its side. Nothing happened. I nosed it up some more and tried to help it along with the rudder.

Then—zowie!—the machine spun, and they don't spin very slowly, either, if they are put in the spin right. Evidently I had put mine in right. At first I was rather at sea as to my exact position [in relation] to the earth. After spinning a couple of times, I came out and looped again, this time much better. By the time I had reached 2,500 feet, I had spun three times and looped as many. The last loop was a peach; couldn't hope for a better one, and I used no power.

When I came down the squadron commander said "Very good," so I feel as though I really can aviate a little now. And oh, how much fun it was.

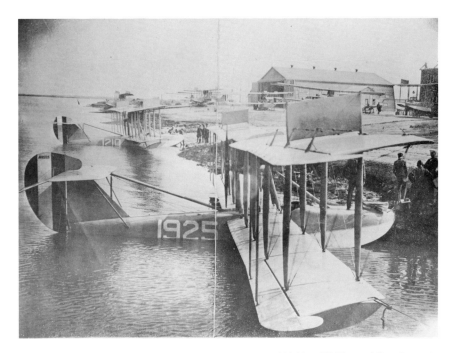

U.S. Navy HS-2L patrol flying boats sit in the water at Cape May, New Jersey. These Curtiss-built planes, powered by 360-horsepower Liberty 12-cylinder engines, were among the types of planes that Russel Merrill flew at Cape May in 1918.

Russel Merrill became Naval Aviator No. 469 on March 12, 1918, when he was presented with his gold wings. In April he was sent to Cape May, New Jersey, for advanced flying instruction. Within months, he was promoted to chief pilot for the station. His rise was both a reflection of flux within a new branch of the wartime Navy and a tribute to his talent as a pilot. His duties included flight instruction and testing repaired planes, as well as the usual naval patrol pilot's military functions, such as bombing and gunnery practice and searching for U-boats.

At Cape May, he flew Curtiss-built R-6 and R-9 twin-pontoon seaplanes and HS-1L and HS-2L flying boats, all powered by Liberty V-12 aero engines. His patrol duties took him over the Barnegat and Atlantic City areas. On

Russel Merrill was promoted to lieutenant junior grade in the Naval Reserve Flying Corps on October 1, 1918.

one occasion he was on the scene twenty minutes after a German submarine torpedoed a schooner off Cape May. He circled the burning ship and dropped a bomb on the water where he saw bubbles. The U-boat escaped.

Once, he was dispatched to the Lowe Willard Fowler aircraft factory at College Point, Long Island, to accept delivery of a new flying boat. It was near evening when the plane was ready, so he flew it down to the Rockaway Naval Air Station to get an early start the following day.

The next morning, he flew up the Hudson River past Grant's Tomb "to say goodbye to New York City," as he put it. He turned back over the city at 2,000 feet, throttled the motor back, and glided about 200 feet over "the Mozart of sky-scrapers," the Woolworth Building, then only five years old.

Suddenly the motor went dead. Merrill had maintained enough altitude to glide to the water, and he set down just off the Battery. He fixed the plane and was in the air again within five minutes.

Merrill was never sent overseas, but by the end of the war, in November 1918, he had been promoted to lieutenant junior grade and was awarded the service chevron. Aviators engaged in hunting enemy craft for three months of the year were eligible for the chevron. He had accumulated 376 hours of flight time. On December 3, he retired from active duty and returned to Des Moines.

Merrill completed his studies at Cornell, earning a degree in chemistry on October 1, 1919. Next came courses in marine piloting, navigation, and boat engineering in San Francisco.

He loved flying and wanted to get into aviation as a business, but the postwar supply of trained pilots vastly exceeded the number of civilian jobs. So he joined the engineering department of Crown Willamette Paper Company, on the Columbia River at Camas, Washington.

At the company he met a vivacious, blue-eyed blonde secretary named Thyra Allen, from nearby Portland, Oregon. A mutual interest immediately blossomed. But in mid-1921, he was promoted to plant manager of the Crown Willamette plant at Floristan, California. He and Thyra stayed in touch.

Earlier that year Merrill's father, Samuel, had died. Then news came that his mother, Fannie, had only twelve months to live. He moved to Palo Alto, California, to spend that last year with her. After his mother died Merrill couldn't wait to get back to the Northwest. In Portland, he helped organize Kern Clay Products, a building materials company, and became general manager.

More importantly, he was reunited with Thyra. The third of four children of the superintendent of schools in Portland, Thyra was high-spirited, made friends easily, and had the knack of reaching out to others and understanding them. Both Thyra and Russel loved life, adventure, and each other. They didn't waste any time in getting married.

Although he was moving up in the business world, Merrill still harbored a strong interest in aviation. He retained his pilot's proficiency by spending fifteen days with the Naval Reserve in San Diego in both 1922 and 1923. He again flew the N-9 primary trainer seaplanes he had flown in 1918 as well as land-based Jennies. He was introduced to a multiengine type, the F-5L flying boat with twin Liberty engines. Both years he flew mail between San Diego and San Pedro for the Navy. But no chance was materializing to return to flying full time.

On April 5, 1925, Merrill saw an advertisement offering a flying boat for sale in Portland. Thyra urged him to investigate. By 1925, she wrote, "aviation had attained a definite standing, and I saw that his thoughts were turning more and more to flying."

The airplane's owner, Roy J. Davis, was an aviation pioneer who now lived in Portland. He had been a pilot and aero-mechanic since 1909, when he built his first airplane, mostly of bamboo. He was Lincoln Beachey's mechanic in 1911 when Beachey raced his Curtiss Pusher airplane against the celebrated Barney Oldfield in his Green Dragon auto racer. Davis was an air observer/gunner in the Lafayette Escadrille for eighteen months until he was disabled. And when he met Merrill, he had been flying commercially out of Portland for more than five years.

Davis had roots in Alaska. His father, Arthur A. Davis, had been construction manager at the New England Fish Company plant in Ketchikan. Davis told Merrill he wouldn't sell his plane, a modified Curtiss Model F flying boat, if he could interest someone in starting an aviation business in Alaska. Merrill was interested. The date of April 5, 1925, was etched permanently in Thyra's memory:

When he came back from the interview, I was in the drawing room playing with Dick. Immediately I sensed a restrained excitement in Russel's manner. He swung his little son high in the air and then turned to me.

"How would you like to go to Alaska?"

Though his lips wore an enigmatic smile, his eyes and the tone of his voice told me that he was serious.

ALASKA

CANADA

ALASKA

CANADA

Anchorage

Kenai

Seward

Latouche

Seldovia

East Chugach Island

Barren Islands

Katalla

Yakutat

Juneau

Telegraph Creek

Devils Thumb

Petersburg

Wrangell

Ketchikan

Bristol Bay

Gulf of Alaska

Ouzinkie

Kodiak

Prince Rupert

Butedale

Ocean Falls

Bella Bella

Queen Charlotte Sound

Alert Bay

town of Alert Bay

Sayward

Vancouver Island

Nanaimo

CANADA

Powell River

Vancouver

UNITED STATES

Seattle

PORTLAND, OREGON

TO ANCHORAGE, ALASKA

Portland

ANYONE NEAR THE **B**ALLARD **L**OCKS IN **S**EATTLE DURING MID-MORNING OF **M**AY 19, 1925, WITNESSED AN UNBELIEVABLE SIGHT. **I**T WAS THE NOISE OF THE FLYING BOAT THAT FIRST ATTRACTED ATTENTION AS IT TAXIED PAST THE **U**NIVERSITY OF **W**ASHINGTON AND THE GAS WORKS ON **L**AKE **U**NION AND NOSED INTO THE SHIP CANAL. **B**UT IT WAS THE VISION OF ITS BIG PROPELLER WHIPPING UP THE WATER BEHIND IT, THE COBWEB OF WIRES AND STRUTS CRISSCROSSING ITS WINGS, AND THE RED, WHITE, AND BLUE-STRIPED RUDDER TURNING FROM SIDE TO SIDE THAT HELD AN ONLOOKER'S GAZE.

Russel Merrill, Roy Davis, and Cyril Krugner had made Seattle from Portland two days before. While the Curtiss F-boat was considered a sprightly climber for its time, its top speed was only 65 miles per hour. The plane always seemed to take forever to get itself off the water. Sure enough, the calm conditions on Lake Washington on the morning of May 19 had again made it too difficult to get airborne. Merrill resorted to the unusual feat of taxiing seven miles through the ship canal to Puget Sound, the airplane passing down through the Ballard Navigation Locks to sea level like some huge, exotic, noisy but earthbound waterbird making its way past groups of moored fishboats.

Once they arrived on the rough, open saltwater of Puget Sound, the choppy water broke the suction under the hull, and the three fliers were up and away in ten minutes. They immediately headed up the east coast of Canada's Vancouver Island. After stops for fuel at Nanaimo and Sayward, they were on their way to windy Cape Scott when oil began streaming from the engine breather pipe and forced them down.

The trio of leather-helmeted airmen in their flying machine looked awfully strange to the Kwakiutl man who happened by in his gas boat. The fliers were able to persuade him to tow them back to Sayward, where they spent the night. No help was available there, so they hired the same native boatman to tow them north through treacherous Johnstone Strait to Alert Bay.

Alert Bay in 1925 was the focal point of the Kwakiutl nation. For the most part, the village existed as it had for thousands of years, with natives living in north-coast longhouses built along a single two-mile-long street and guarded by totem poles large and small, some colored with soft earth pigments, others garishly covered with house paint. But the white tower of a government radio station, along with a number of modern-looking warehouses along the waterfront, told the personnel of the Roy J. Davis Airplane Company that help was available. Repairs cost them a couple of days, but on April 24 the fliers were once more on their way.

Merrill's Navy training in night flying paid off as they tried to make up for lost time. They arrived at Bella Bella that day, stayed overnight at a cannery, and then made for Prince Rupert, ninety miles south of Ketchikan, Alaska. From Prince Rupert, flying in the dark, they crossed the Alaska line in fog and rain, navigating the last stretch by hugging the east coast of Prince of Wales Island. At midnight they set down for a few hours' rest in the little flying boat as it nestled in a cove like a storm petrel. Miserably cramped in the cockpit, they were happy to take off at sunrise.

At 5:30 a.m. May 26, almost within sight of their destination, the cough of the motor warned them that their fuel supply was exhausted. Forced down once again, engine quiet and propeller still, they were towed behind a barge into the harbor of Ketchikan, where they moored the airplane. They had made it to Alaska.

Wearing leather flight gear, Russel Merrill walks toward the flying boat at a beach on a trip to Anchorage in 1925. Merrill—along with Roy Davis and Cyril Krugner—had flown the Curtiss Model F flying boat earlier that year from Portland, Oregon, to Alaska.

Davis's dream of barnstorming in Alaska was inspired by the example of Roy F. Jones, a former Army pilot from Seattle, and Gerald J. Smith, his mechanic, who arrived in Ketchikan on July 17, 1922, in the ex-Navy Curtiss MF flying boat *Northbird.* Their arrival generated excitement that amazed the tired fliers. But the town's love affair with aviation was interrupted in August of 1923 when *Northbird,* driven by powerful mountain downdrafts, nosed into nearby Heckman Lake and was destroyed.

So when Ketchikan awoke May 26, 1925, to find a near-duplicate of *Northbird* moored on the waterfront, it quickly became clear that the airplane's absence for almost two years had only made Ketchikan's heart grow fonder. The townspeople thronged to welcome the fliers and offer their services. A float was assigned to them free of charge. Soon the aviators had more requests for flights than they could accommodate.

Ketchikan is located amid one of the greatest concentrations of timber, mining, and fishing resources on Earth, none of which had ever been adequately surveyed. One of Merrill's first services to Ketchikan was to use his aerial camera to photograph the town and its setting. His first charter, arranged during the first day there, was with a prospector. In time, flying miners and trappers in and out of their territories became one of Merrill's main commercial activities in Ketchikan.

Merrill saw another potential source of revenue swimming below his wings as he flew barnstorming passengers around Ketchikan. From the air he could see the size and direction of a fish run and direct boats to intercept it. Merrill was hired to spot salmon runs for a Ketchikan cannery, saving the cannery time and increasing its catches.

Merrill's telegram to his wife inviting her to come north was so enthusiastic that Thyra took a boat to Ketchikan from Portland and got there faster than he had by air. She and the boys were there in a week.

After long days in the air mixing intense up-and-down barnstorming with his first charter flights, Merrill still found the energy to paint the interior of the small house he had found for the family. When Thyra saw the cottage, which in her view had every convenience, her apprehensions about the rigors of life in the Far North evaporated.

Much more social than her husband, Thyra enjoyed spending her days

Pilot Russel Merrill prepares to take a passenger up in the Curtiss flying boat—the one airplane of the Roy J. Davis Airplane Company—in southeastern Alaska in late July 1925. The plane bore U.S. Lighthouse Service motorboat registration number 475U as there was no civil aircraft number system at the time.

poking into odd corners of curio stores and wandering about the steeply graded streets of Ketchikan. While Russel was an important figure in Ketchikan from the moment he arrived, Thyra added to the Merrill family's popularity almost overnight. They were a team.

Word of aviators Merrill and Davis spread quickly northward, and invitations to take their airplane to other southeastern Alaska towns—Wrangell, Petersburg, Juneau—were piling up. On July 1, after promising to return to Ketchikan for Fourth of July festivities, Merrill and Davis flew to Petersburg, 120 miles farther up the Alaskan Panhandle.

A small fishing town built on piles over mud flats, Petersburg had never seen an airplane, and the townspeople greeted it with a standing ovation. The F-boat was used hard: it made innumerable ten-minute hops, and an enterprising engineer named Harold Waller, involved in building the Blind Slough Power Project fifteen miles from Petersburg, hired the F-boat to travel to and from the site.

Merrill and Davis returned on July 3 to Ketchikan, where Merrill's family waited anxiously for him. Dick, age two, was starry-eyed with excitement; he had been promised his first airplane ride.

On the Fourth, Dick got his flight along with many others. Late in the day the cam shaft broke, ending the flying festivities and convincing Merrill that the engine needed a thorough overhaul after all its accumulated band-aid repairs.

On July 16 he took the plane with its overhauled engine up for a test flight. At 600 feet above the harbor, the F-boat unaccountably went into a spin. Merrill was calm and detached as he worked the wheel, pedals, and throttle, trying to regain control. But he had previously said it would be almost impossible to bring the flying boat out of a spin. His single matter-of-fact thought as the plane spun downward was, "Well, there goes another good aviator."

But he did stop the spin and regain control—only fifty feet from the water. He did not say what caused the spin, but people watching the flight were thrilled. They thought he was doing aerobatics for their entertainment.

Two days later Krugner departed for the States. It wasn't necessary to keep a mechanic since the plane couldn't be flown when it was undergoing repairs so Merrill could just as well service it himself.

With Krugner gone and Davis involved in other business commitments, Merrill was left to make a flight to Wrangell and Juneau alone. This posed no special problem. For warming up the flying boat, he needed someone to keep the nose facing the float, and a second person had to be ready to turn the plane around. But he could always find someone at the docks eager to help.

However, he also knew that Thyra would want to go. Russel took great pride in teaching her to fly, giving her time at the controls whenever they were alone. He praised her ability to their friends. His way of inviting her along was to say, "I'll need someone to help me on the docks. Would you consider going with me on this trip?" Thyra liked her husband's gracious custom of making it appear that the advantage to him was greater than to the favored one.

ON JULY 16 MERRILL TOOK THE CURTISS FLYING BOAT WITH ITS OVERHAULED ENGINE UP FOR A TEST FLIGHT. AT 600 FEET ABOVE THE HARBOR, THE F-BOAT UNACCOUNTABLY WENT INTO A SPIN. MERRILL WAS CALM AND DETACHED AS HE WORKED THE WHEEL, PEDALS, AND THROTTLE, TRYING TO REGAIN CONTROL.

IT WAS AN UNFORGETTABLE FLIGHT. RUSSEL AND THYRA PASSED OVER PEAK AFTER PEAK. THEY BARELY SKIMMED THE SUMMITS, TO BE SWEPT DOWNWARD BY BREATHTAKING DOWN-WASHES IN THE DARK, SHADOWED LEE OF EACH MOUNTAIN AND CAUGHT UP BY UPDRAFTS CLIMBING THE BRIGHT, WINDWARD SIDE OF THE NEXT SLOPE.

On a mid-July afternoon, with rain that showed no sign of letting up, Russel and Thyra embarked on a kind of soggy second honeymoon that almost didn't get off the water. Finding no breeze, they taxied for an hour trying to get airborne, then decided to circumnavigate the island to more open water. It was a glorified speedboat ride until the engine overheated; then they would slow down to cool it. They finally caught a swift little current of air and were off. It was 9 p.m. and still raining hard. At the aircraft's cruising speed the raindrops struck them in the open cockpit like hailstones. They were forced back to Ketchikan.

This was Thyra's first experience with a night landing on water, and she was worried as they descended between the mountains and the island. Without direct light to illuminate the water's surface, she and Russel seemed to be descending into a dark void with no idea when they would hit bottom. Although she could not distinguish the water at all, Russel made a perfect landing and pulled up to the float, where well-wishers had already gathered to meet them. The couple clambered out of the craft dripping wet. Thyra noted that nothing like that ever daunted Russel, and she felt exhilarated herself.

Two days later they finally started their trip on a clear morning that, in retrospect, made her grateful to have been in the old Curtiss flying boat, with its motor and propeller behind them, so they could enjoy clean air and an unobstructed view ahead. Soon, though, the age of their antiquated kite made itself felt. As they approached Clarence Strait, the motor began to hiss. The fuel gauge did not register; Russel landed in the channel to investigate. Thyra steered the plane in circles while Russel examined the engine. A leak in the intake manifold was allowing water into the engine oil. Russel plugged it as well as he could. They took off again, were forced down once more, and took off once more: up, down, up—and away. This time the stopgap held, and they arrived in Wrangell about noon.

Although it was hardly necessary to announce their presence to a small town witnessing its first aircraft, Russel and Thyra circled several times, in the barnstormer's style. From the air they were charmed by the peacefulness of the old town, drowsing in its garden setting under the midday sunshine that emphasized the rich colors of the totem poles along the board streets and hillside paths. After the landing, the townspeople were impressed to see a woman helping to handle the aircraft.

The Curtiss flying boat owned by Roy Davis taxis on inland coastal waters on the way to Anchorage in 1925. The plane was a war surplus U.S. Navy standard flying boat trainer. This Model F (revised) cost $7,500 to produce and sold unused on the postwar market at $1,750.

A small lumber mill operated on Wrangell's waterfront, and Russel found it difficult to avoid the surface debris from it each time he taxied out from the float. During the second day there, he felt a minor jolt and heard a ripping sound as he was taking off. A piece of shingle had struck the tail assembly. That ended flying for the day. Responding to the town's keen disappointment, the Merrills set to work at once to repair the damage.

They worked all night. In the absence of cotton or linen, Thyra resorted to buying muslin. While Russel prepared the horizontal stabilizer and rudder frames for re-covering, his wife washed and dried the cloth to shrink it.

It was painstaking work to fit the cloth to the frame by lamplight and sew it absolutely smooth and tight. Next came the job of applying the dope, a pigmented filler and lacquer that protects the cotton skin of stick and wire airplanes and makes it tight as a drum—coat after coat at half-hour intervals for drying. Then came paint and shellac. Breathing the fumes of kerosene, turpentine, and banana oil made them giddy and a little sick, but they were determined to be back in the air by noon. By 11 a.m. the tail was ready for reassembly. While Russel put it back together, Thyra had some food prepared and brought it to the dock. The Merrills were back in business.

After a week in Wrangell, Petersburg's accumulated requests for a return visit became more insistent. Thyra selected their route. They flew up the Stikine River to Telegraph Creek, British Columbia, over a rugged landscape that struck her as enchanted. For Thyra, it would be a temptation to travel there, prospecting not for gold but for beauty. Turning west from there, they flew directly into the sun for Petersburg, over the alabaster and blue Baird and Patterson glaciers. To the right were countless peaks, with the fabled Devils Thumb in the distance. They would be back.

The welcoming committee at Petersburg was disappointed to learn that Russel and Thyra would be lunching with Harold Waller. After a fine meal, Russel agreed to fly the civil engineer to the Blind Slough Power Project once more and call for him that evening. Most of the afternoon was spent barnstorming, and by the time Russel returned from the power plant site, dusk was settling over water and town. They decided to make one last flight this day, just the two of them, across the bay, over the glaciers and as close to Devils Thumb as they dared go.

It was an unforgettable flight. They passed over peak after peak. They barely skimmed the summits, to be swept downward by breathtaking downwashes in the dark, shadowed lee of each mountain and caught up by updrafts climbing the bright, windward side of the next slope. Far down the bay, a silvery Alaska passenger boat trailed a dark banner of smoke. Up in the hazy sky, Russel and Thyra were prolonging a perfect day already ended on the ground.

Suddenly, crossing yet another peak, they were struck breathless at the glacier that looked to be just below their wings but was more than a mile below: a giant checkerboard in diaphanous blue and white squares on a wide table flanked by mountains, seamed with crevasses of celestial blue. Looking up, they saw Devils Thumb, soaring high into the sky.

Now the sun had melted away into the thickening haze, leaving only a glow on the horizon. They realized they were thoroughly chilled. Russel throttled back the motor and glided three miles so quietly that friends awaiting their return saw them faintly outlined against the sky without hearing the airplane as it slid into the harbor at Petersburg.

As gratifying as their welcomes had been in Wrangell and Petersburg, Russel and Thyra still were unprepared for Juneau's excited response to their flying machine. Looking for a likely spot to touch down, they circled the town. They also flew over the huge nearby Mendenhall Glacier. Aware that Juneau's population was smaller than Ketchikan's, they were surprised by the impressive looks of the plant of the Alaska Juneau Gold Mining Company, which dominated the town from its steep mountainside aerie. Russel and Thyra's overflight of Juneau ended the championship baseball game of that season as fans and players alike watched them from the ground. It was Sunday, and the crowd was three deep for at least a block at the docks where the flying boat moored.

Barnstorming over Juneau acquainted Russel with one of the hazards of

AS GRATIFYING AS THEIR WELCOMES HAD BEEN IN WRANGELL AND PETERSBURG, RUSSEL AND THYRA STILL WERE UNPREPARED FOR JUNEAU'S EXCITED RESPONSE TO THEIR FLYING MACHINE.

Roy Davis's Curtiss flying boat hangs on a hoist at Juneau in July 1925. The plane's engine had 50 horsepower more than the standard Model F, but Davis and Russel Merrill still had repeated difficulty getting the plane airborne in smooth water. Takeoffs were easier in choppy water, which served to break the suction between hull and water.

flight in the area. Flying over glaciers presented hazards because of their effects on the air above them. Russel had heard of the destructive Taku winds that occasionally rise without warning on the glacier and sweep down on the town with destructive force. According to native folklore, the winds were the breaths of evil spirits.

The townspeople were anxious to see Alaska's capital and the nearby Mendenhall and Taku glaciers from the air, and he was not concerned one clear day when he took two girls for a pleasure ride over the harbor and town. Suddenly, as Russel and his young passengers flew around the outskirts of Juneau, a Taku swooped down with startling force.

It was impossible to land in the immediate vicinity; the hull would have been smashed against the water. Unable to gain altitude, Russel flew around at an altitude of fifty feet, looking for relief from the downblast. The long dump from the mine offered some protection, and he finally set down on the water on its lee side, fuel tank bone dry. The girls were not in the least frightened; indeed, they said they were thrilled by the adventure.

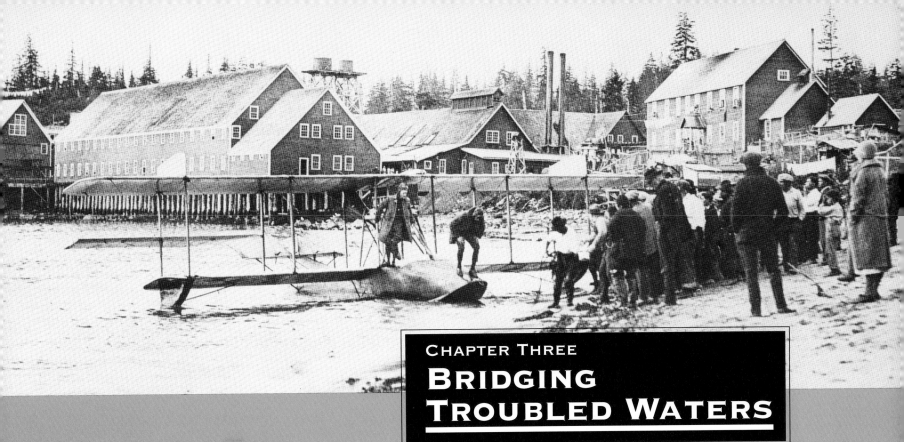

Chapter Three
BRIDGING
TROUBLED WATERS

Gelles and I walked back to the plane (the Curtiss

Model F flying boat), to find that the wind had

broken one of the lines and had turned her on her

nose and back. . . . Until 3 a.m. we watched the plane

gradually go to pieces as the tide came in!

— Russel Merrill, in a letter to his wife, Thyra, relating the
loss of his plane on East Chugach Island early on the
morning of September 5, 1925

"WE STARTED OUT AT 9 O'CLOCK WITH THE SKY CLEAR" IS THE MATTER-OF-FACT BEGINNING TO RUSSEL MERRILL'S LOGBOOK ACCOUNT OF A FLIGHT THAT WAS ANYTHING BUT ROUTINE: HIS FIRST EXPLORATION FLIGHT IN ALASKA.

I flew close to the water to conserve gasoline. After about 50 miles, the fog began to roll in. Soon it lay thick on the water, forcing me to rise. Before long it was all around us, and I hunted for holes. But as we came through each light spot, we were just as badly off as before, because the fog was everywhere. We climbed and descended and climbed again. We were using gas up fast. After an hour, with fog still dense, Roy poured in the first can of reserve gas.

That day—Saturday, August 1, 1925—Russel Merrill and Roy Davis set out to fly the 750 miles from Juneau to Seward over the Gulf of Alaska, a brave undertaking for two men in a frail flying boat with a single small motor. Although they chose the month with the best weather over the gulf, they still had to contend with fog and the possibility of strong winds that could blow them out to sea. Should a storm arise or engine trouble strike, there would be little chance of survival in the frigid waters. Their emergency equipment consisted of two extra cans of gasoline and some sandwiches.

Davis had returned to Juneau from the States on July 28 to help with the intensive but quiet final planning for the flight. They sought no publicity from a press that was only too happy to dramatize their every takeoff. Their vision of aviation in the north foresaw future flights over such dangerous waters as everyday events. To invite attention and then fail might hurt their cause in the eyes of future passengers.

The gulf had been spanned by air before, but in a manner that under-

Overleaf: Roy Davis and Russel Merrill arrive at Yakutat village on August 1, 1925, during their historic crossing of the Gulf of Alaska from Juneau to Seward.

lined the risks Merrill and Davis were accepting. Four new U.S. Army airplanes—400-horsepower, ninety-mile-an-hour Douglas World Cruisers built especially for the expedition—had crossed from Sitka to Seward in April 1924 on one leg of their six-month around-the-world flight. They were supported by their own Air Service mechanics and had rescue and logistics backing from U.S. Navy ships stationed along the route. Their achievement was as much a triumph of military organization as the pilots' airmanship and caused a sensation at each settlement they passed. The equalizer between this interservice juggernaut and the lonely two-man effort was the piloting skill of Russel Merrill.

Merrill and Davis were very much on their own on what was to be a survey flight to prove that regular commercial flights were possible across a body of water still considered by pilots to be one of the least predictable in the world. Rescue services, radio-beam navigation, and up-to-the-minute weather forecasts were many years in the future. Merrill and Davis would make the flight in carefully plotted hops, according to the calculations of the F-boat's fuel and oil consumption that Merrill constantly updated in his logbook.

The fuel they took on at the Standard Oil dock on the Juneau waterfront would give them a range of 300 miles. They planned to refuel at Yakutat, which sits at the southern end of an isthmus bordered to the west by a large bay. If they overshot the isolated town, they would be back over frigid waters with the gas gauge trembling near empty. Merrill's log continues:

I kept close to our compass course in spite of the constant losing and taking of altitude. We figured we must be drawing close to Yakutat; we were so low on gas that we had to put in our last can.

REFUELING THE CURTISS FLYING BOAT IN THE AIR WAS AS HAZARDOUS AS IT SOUNDS. BOTH FLIERS WERE OUTDOORS IN THE OPEN COCKPIT, BUNDLED UP IN LONG SHEEPSKIN COATS, BOOTS, MITTS, HELMETS, AND GOGGLES. ONLY A SMALL WINDSHIELD PROTECTED THEM FROM THE BLAST OF THE AIRSTREAM. NOW DAVIS HAD TO CLIMB OUT OF THE COCKPIT TO REACH THE GASOLINE TANK.

Pouring gasoline from a can into the gas tank while the plane was in the air was as hazardous as it sounds, but not especially unusual. Both fliers were outdoors in the open cockpit to begin with, bundled up in long sheep-skin coats, boots, mitts, helmets, and goggles. Only a small windshield protected them from the blast of the airstream. Now Davis had to climb out of the cockpit to reach the gasoline tank, with the wind threatening to tear him from the plane.

First, Davis reached up with his left hand to grasp the F-boat's Goodier strut, a varnished thick spruce member running diagonally between the two men from the radiator mount above and behind them down to the lower forward hull structure. Then Davis pulled himself up and was pressed against the strut by the gale-force wind, now at his back. He reached over the top wing, at about shoulder height, to remove the filler cap from the airfoil-shaped tank on the top of the wing with his gloved right hand. Merrill handed up the gas can, and Davis, scarf flapping and one hand gripping the Goodier strut for dear life, poured in the precious fuel. Done with the harrowing task, Davis slipped back into the relative safety and comfort of the cockpit.

More than anything else, the airmen were pounded from all sides by noise: the unmuffled throb of the engine above them, the chopping of the air by the propeller, the drumming of the doped-fabric skin, the reverberating whistle of the wind through the struts and vibrating wires holding the plane together. The sounds combined into a numbing barrage as they droned along in their cold white world.

The Curtiss F-boat was designed before instrument panels became essential parts of aircraft. A few engine instruments were mounted here and there, such as the tachometer and the oil-pressure and water-temperature gauges. A clear section of the overhead gas line with a float inside told them

The Curtiss Model F flying boat sits on the beach at Seward after Roy Davis and Russel Merrill's crossing of the Gulf of Alaska August 1–3, 1925.

their fuel level. These crude instruments confirmed in various ways what their ears told them through their leather helmets: that the motor was running and just might continue doing so.

They had nothing but Merrill's wristwatch, the engine tachometer, and the steady throb of the motor to suggest how far they had come.

As for what their airplane was doing in the sky, they relied to a great deal on the wind in their faces and the seats of their pants to tell them they were straightened up and flying right. An inclinometer, which worked like a carpenter's level, showed whether the plane was flying with a wingtip low. A string tied to the wire running from the nose to the midpoint of the upper

The Curtiss flying boat floats next to the shore at Lawning Resort, Kenai Lake, on August 7, 1925, after a day trip from Seward. From left are pilot Russel Merrill, Alaska Nellie, and William Patterson. Alaska Nellie owned a nearby lodge and eating establishment.

wing—plus the wind in their faces—told them whether they were side-slipping. A simple barometer measured air pressure, which decreases at higher elevations and thereby indicates altitude.

Not for another three years or so would blind-flying instruments, such as the turn-and-bank indicator, be generally available. Despite the belief of most pioneer pilots that they could sense the attitudes of their planes at night or in dense fog, the deadly truth was they could fly only seven to ten minutes without dipping a wing, diving slightly, or turning without being aware of it. Trying to fly blind for longer than ten minutes without the help of special instruments often led to disaster. Merrill's log resumes:

Luckily, the fog began to lift. We had deviated surprisingly little from our set course, when we came out close to the beach. Directly before us was a group of houses. We had made the halfway point!

Merrill's Navy training and pilot's instincts—his ability to fly by the seat of his pants—are what got him and Davis to Yakutat in one piece. Yakutat was not quite halfway to Seward, but they knew they were over the worst part of the trip when they arrived there at 5 p.m. that Saturday. They stayed overnight.

The next day they spent four hours taxiing before they were able to coax the plane off the water and back into the air. Flying through fog, three hours later the F-boat appeared at the Chilkat oil refinery at Katalla to refuel and spend the night. Monday they flew to Seward, refueling at Latouche along the way. The fog had cleared entirely by the time they flew over Harding's Entrance and into Resurrection Bay, Seward's harbor, at 9 p.m. August 3. The pioneering flight took a total of ten hours and twenty minutes of flying time.

The Curtiss flying boat of the Roy J. Davis Airplane Company was the first airplane to ever fly into Anchorage. Roy Davis and Russel Merrill landed unannounced at 8:30 p.m. on August 20, 1925. Carrying Frank Murphy, a passenger from Seward, they set down on Cook Inlet and tied up at the city dock.

Businessman Gus Gelles, a great advocate of aviation at Anchorage, chartered the flying boat for a bold flight to Kodiak in August 1925, piloted by Russel Merrill. Gelles, known as a formal dresser, poses in relatively informal attire in this photo taken while his business suit was being cleaned following his Kodiak adventure.

While the men of the Roy J. Davis Airplane Company had proven that crossing the moody Gulf of Alaska with a lone airplane was possible, they realized that the everyday use of the route would not be practical without more reliable equipment for navigation and blind flying.

Merrill and Davis barnstormed for two weeks in Seward, showing off the flying boat and earning money by taking people on rides. Then they made history by flying into Anchorage. From Seward they flew over the Kenai Peninsula, up Cook Inlet, and to Anchorage, with a passenger from Seward, Frank Murphy, also aboard.

Few residents who heard them approaching on the evening of August 20, 1925, recognized the sound as an airplane. The flying boat circled the city twice and then landed at 8:30, becoming the first airplane ever to fly into Anchorage. (Two planes had flown briefly in Anchorage, one in 1922 and one 1924, but both had been shipped in and assembled there.) The *Anchorage Times* promptly covered their arrival and announced that the seaplane would take passengers up in the air from the city dock starting the next day. Barnstorming and advertising were under way.

Merrill's first outing from Anchorage was anything but routine. He spent two dog days in late August trying to lift off the water for the charter trip to Kodiak before finally departing in a southwesterly direction, expecting to be away only two days.

The charter passenger for Kodiak was Gus Gelles, an entrepreneur who had wired ahead to his clients and expected an enthusiastic reception when he stepped out of his hired flying machine and started taking orders. Dressed in new oxfords and a new suit of clothes, he was eager to cover more territory more quickly than ever before as the Alaska representative of the National Grocery and Brunswick Balk wholesale concerns. Gelles brought along order and sample books and carried a sack lunch. He was also one of the founders of Alaska Glacier Tours, and he planned to scout the Kenai Peninsula for hunting and fishing sites.

Gelles, Davis, and Merrill flew down to Kenai on Monday, August 24. After several days of mechanical problems and false stops and starts, the men found themselves that weekend in the town of Seldovia on the southern end of the Kenai Peninsula. A letter Russel wrote to Thyra tells the story of the rest of this trip, which turned out to be extended and full of adventure:

This was the first plane in Seldovia, and at $10 a trip we took in $200, despite the fact an aileron control wire broke while

Before its flight to Kodiak, the Curtiss flying boat waits at Seldovia at the end of August 1925.

Pilot Russel Merrill and business-man Gus Gelles arrived at Kodiak just after 11 p.m. on August 31, 1925, in the Curtiss flying boat, the first airplane the town had ever seen. With his plane short on gas, and flying low to see by the hazy light of the moon, Merrill managed to land safely. The entire town turned out to greet them in the middle of the night.

I was in the air with a passenger and I managed a poor landing cross wind with one wing hitting the water before the boat.

Monday [August 31], Gelles and I tried practically all day to get off for Kodiak, but it was too calm until just as we were coming back into the bay. Here we struck a breeze and took off at seven in the evening. About eight we were off Barren Islands; it was pretty dark and getting darker and cloudier. At eight-thirty we sighted Marmot Island, but nearing land we found too much fog, so we continued on our course to Kodiak. At nine the moon gave quite a bit of light and the weather began to clear. Then we sighted the lights of a town. We knew it was not Kodiak, but as we had very little gas, we landed, between the cannery and the timber.

The town turned out to be Ouzinkie, about 12 miles from Kodiak. The people at the cannery gave us a feed, and we bought five gallons of gas. We started on at 11 p.m. by the diffused light of the moon. Ten minutes later we were over Kodiak, flying low, trying to see land in the hazy light. There were many boats, and as we maneuvered about, the plane missed a buoy by a few scant inches.

The entire town of Kodiak turned out to greet us. There had never been a plane there before.

The following day [September 1] a terrific gale came up. I had to spend that evening repairing the oil pressure gauge, as it had gone out of commission from taxiing in the afternoon. The next morning we got off on a "wooly" [localized gust of wind], circled the town and the radio station, and then started for Seldovia.

About five miles from the wireless station, the motor began to miss and we turned back. The motor died in a minute or two, and we had just enough altitude to get within a quarter mile of the station.

The gasoline pump wasn't working. A launch came out and towed us in. We were invited to dinner at an orphanage, and enjoyed it immensely. After dinner I took out the gas pump and fixed it. We tried to go, but as we could not get off, we taxied back to Kodiak. No luck the next day, either.

Friday morning [September 4] at 9:50 we took off with a good wind and fine weather, heading for Seldovia. The further we got, the harder the wind blew, and the weather thickened. When we were about five miles off Marmot Island, I came down to see if we could fly under the little clouds floating beneath us. Mountainous, whitecapped waves were breaking high and a stiff breeze was blowing over the water.

As the wind was favorable, I decided to go over the fog. We climbed to 1,500 feet and got over some of it, but it only grew thicker. Soon it was all fog, we could see nothing else. I kept close watch of our balance and steered *a fairly straight course by the compass, climbing all the time. The Barren Islands were the only land near; since the highest peak there is less than 2,000 feet, we were soon over that altitude. We were in the fog for twenty minutes, and at 4,000 feet finally got over it, but could see no land.*

Soon I saw what I took to be the north shore of Cook Inlet. According to this, we were headed too far out to sea, so for half an hour we flew further in. Finally I saw a clear spot in the fog and water under us, which relieved me somewhat; then we saw a snowcapped mountain peak ahead. Just before reaching the mountain, there was another hole in the fog which showed a shore line. I came down to 700 feet and found that we were some 40 miles from Seldovia, with quite misty weather and a 40-mile wind that we had to buck. It seemed like ages before we got out of the little bay we were over and out to sea once more.

We were quite near East Chugach Island, where I knew there was a fox farm. (Dwyer, the jailer at Seldovia, had told us that his wife was on the place and that we would be able to get some gas from her. He had given us a box of candy to deliver to her.) Our gasoline overflow did not register, although I kept a close watch of it for fifteen minutes.

Consequently I thought we had better land at the island. I came around in the lee of the shore, making a perfect landing in very rough water. The first breaker filled the tail and the plane started taking water over the nose, so we came up to the most protected part of the beach we could find. I tried to keep the plane headed straight in to the beach; but in spite of all I could do, the waves broke one flipper, the rudder, and the other flipper.

We kept the motor going until the tide was high. Gelles went in search of the house, and when the tide had partially ebbed, I tied one wing to a good-sized log and the nose to a larger one. Then, soaking wet, I walked over a mile to the house where Mrs. Dwyer had a hot meal ready for us, and delivered the box of candy to her. After eating, I lay down for an hour, as I was pretty well tuckered out.

After my rest, Gelles and I walked back to the plane, to find that the wind had broken one of the lines and had turned her on her nose and back, lifting the other log. The top wing was smashed in a couple of places. We saw that we couldn't save the wings when the next tide came in, so we chopped away a part of the upper one

Little was left of the one airplane of the Roy J. Davis Airplane Company after being demolished by waves on the beach at East Chugach Island early on the morning of September 5, 1925. Russel Merrill made a forced landing September 4 on a return flight from Kodiak with businessman Gus Gelles as the Curtiss flying boat, low on fuel, bucked a strong head wind. In this photo, Gus Gelles is holding the shovel; standing to the right is Mrs. Dwyer, who lived nearby and helped the downed fliers.

and took the motor out and hauled it above high water. This was some little job for the two of us.

Until 3 a.m. we watched the plane gradually go to pieces as the tide came in!

Saturday we righted the boat after taking off what was left of the wings. We watched for passing boats but had no luck. On Sunday we got a bed sheet from Mrs. Dwyer and flagged a small boat with a crew of five men who had been caught in the same storm. They were in a little dinghy patched with oil cans. Gelles went on board and was taken to Seldovia for help; he said that the "crew was rough and the weather rougher." Two of the crew stayed to help me pull what was left of the plane above high water and to carry the motor further in, where we covered it up.

This afternoon the S.S. Admiral Evans came for me and put ashore a lifeboat with eight men. Gelles, after taking a small gas boat out from Seldovia, had caught her at Graham Island. . . . It seemed mighty good to get aboard her. . . . Must get an hour's sleep, as it is two-thirty and we are getting in early.

How did Gelles react to his eventful sales and scouting trip?

"It was a wonderful experience and one I wouldn't have missed for a whole lot. I never saw so many beautiful lakes and such wonderful scenery in my life."

Still attired in his suit and oxfords, and carrying his book of new orders, Gelles told a reporter the only thing he had lost in the wreck of the F-boat was his lunch, uneaten in all the excitement. He said he had accomplished as detailed an inventory of hunting grounds on the Kenai Peninsula as he could possibly have wished. He gained weight on the trip and "never felt better in my life."

"Am sending some blueberries from East Chugach Island for you," an upbeat Merrill concluded in his letter to Thyra from the *Admiral Evans.* "And so this is the end of the trail—one trail. This Kodiak trip has indeed been a hard one; but things will be different from now on."

CHAPTER FOUR

INTO THE FUTURE: 1926

GUESS YOU KNOW THAT I'D RATHER FLY IN

ALASKA AND LIVE ON BEANS THAN FLY DOWN

HERE AND OWN A ROLLS ROYCE.

— RUSSEL MERRILL,
IN A LETTER WRITTEN FROM THE PACIFIC
NORTHWEST, ACCEPTING THE JOB OF CHIEF
PILOT FOR NEWLY FORMED ANCHORAGE AIR
TRANSPORT, INC., IN 1926

AFTER LOSING THEIR CURTISS FLYING BOAT, RUSSEL MERRILL AND ROY DAVIS RENAMED THEIR OPERATION THE ALASKA-OREGON-WASHINGTON AIRPLANE COMPANY AND SEEMED POISED FOR BETTER THINGS IN 1926. THEY PUT IN A BUSY OFF-SEASON IN SEATTLE, PORTLAND, AND SAN FRANCISCO NEGOTIATING CONTRACTS FOR MAIL AND PASSENGER FLIGHTS BETWEEN SEVEN CANNERIES OPERATING ON BRISTOL BAY AND THE COMPANY'S NEW BASE AT SEWARD.

Bristol Bay is the gulf northwest of the Alaska Peninsula and is home to one of the largest fisheries in the world. Seward, the destination of Merrill and Davis's Gulf of Alaska flight less than a year before, was an ideal choice as their base of operations. Rail and steamship terminals were located there, and the town was enthusiastic about the idea of becoming an aviation center as well. All the Alaska-Oregon-Washington Airplane Company lacked was an airplane.

In retrospect their old F-boat looked a lot better than any plane they could get to replace it. They located a Curtiss Oriole floatplane with a K-6 engine. Introduced in 1919 to sell for nearly $10,000, the Oriole should have been a considerable improvement over the F-boat, a pre-World War I design. They bought this one for much less money because the Curtiss factory slashed prices when the expected postwar mass market for new airplanes did not materialize.

Merrill test-flew the Oriole May 14 from Swan Island Lagoon on the Willamette River near Portland, Oregon, and thought it handled fairly well in the air although it was underpowered. He had misgivings about its high center of gravity above the wood floats, which made it tricky to handle on the water. These concerns proved moot when Merrill and Davis struck a

Overleaf: Russel Merrill stands on the beach at Swan Island Lagoon outside Portland, Oregon, with the Curtiss Oriole floatplane he and Roy Davis planned to fly to Alaska in 1926. The craft was later damaged during testing so they did not use it.

submerged log just prior to liftoff on a test flight May 21 and the aircraft nosed over in the water, destroying its left pontoon and wings.

The search for a replacement took them north to Vancouver, British Columbia. Major Donald R. MacLaren, a dapper Royal Flying Corps World War I ace and now pilot-manager of Pacific Airways Ltd., was selling a war-surplus Aeromarine 40B flying boat that had never been used. It had a 180-horsepower Hispano-Suiza engine and a spare 150-horsepower Hisso. The Aeromarine was quite similar to the Curtiss F-boat overall but was designed to carry three passengers in addition to the pilot.

Merrill and Davis assembled the plane at a machine shop on Granville Island in Vancouver and flight-tested it June 21, only a month after the Oriole crashed. The Hispano-Suiza overheated so badly they replaced the standard radiator with a larger one. It was not for another six days, late in the afternoon of June 27, that the two felt safe enough with the Aeromarine to leave Vancouver, heading back to Alaska.

In a letter to Thyra, Merrill detailed the intricacies of coaxing the Aeromarine along on the flight to Alaska:

We started from Vancouver June 27th rather late in the afternoon and landed at Powell River just after dark, speed 60 knots wide open. The next morning I broke the crankshaft mechanism trying to crank the motor. On taking it apart we found that it was not made to fit this engine. We had a new part made at a paper mill machine shop.

We tried to start for Alert Bay the same day but broke the camshaft drive eight miles out. We landed and taxied to shore on one bank of the motor and replaced the broken part with one from the spare parts we brought with us. When we got away from shore (after dark) the air was too rough to

WE SIGHTED A BOAT AND LANDED HALF A MILE FROM HER. AS WE STARTED TO TAXI UP TO HER, WE RAN OUT OF GAS. WE LIGHTED TWO DISTRESS SIGNALS, BUT THE BOAT MERELY PUT HER SEARCHLIGHT ON US AND WENT HER OWN WAY!

— LETTER FROM RUSSEL MERRILL, DESCRIBING THE DIFFICULTIES OF PILOTING AN AEROMARINE FLYING BOAT UP THE BRITISH COLUMBIA COAST IN 1926

Drawings show the Aeromarine 40B
flying boat that Russel Merrill and
Roy Davis flew to Alaska in the
summer of 1926. It was a never-used
war surplus flying boat powered by a
180-horsepower eight-cylinder
Hispano-Suiza engine.

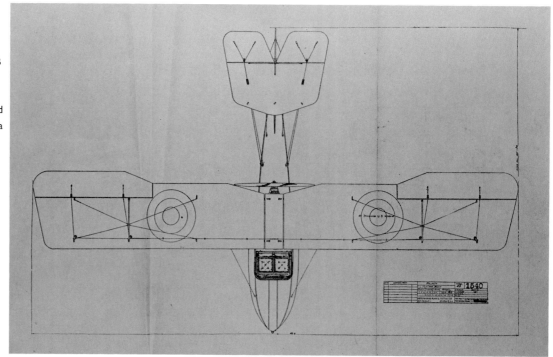

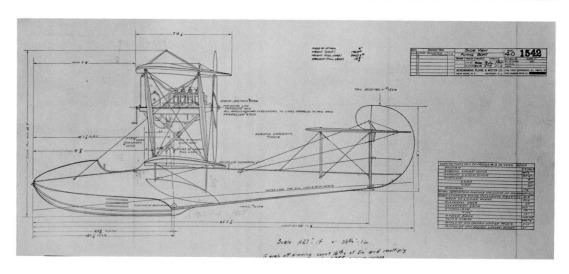

fly back to Powell River, so taxied there which took three hours.

The next day the boat would not take off until some water was pumped out of the forward part of the hull. We flew twelve miles out from Powell River when the motor slowed due to plug trouble. The weather was pretty rough but we finally found shelter at a logging camp on Hernando Island and stayed there overnight. The following morning we started for Alert Bay; the motor ran all right throttled back a little. We struck strong head winds and had to land at Sayward for gas and oil.

After carrying twenty gallons of gas over a mile to the plane we left for Alert Bay. The air just off the water was extremely rough. At one point we dropped from two hundred feet to forty feet—for an instant it looked as though we wouldn't stop short of the water! Out from shore the air was smoother, but there was a fifty-mile wind against us, so we had to return, landing among the "bumps" [waves] without mishap.

July 1st we flew to Alert Bay against a strong head wind without incident except the motor missed some as we were about to land. After cleaning the carburetor and buying gas we started for Bella Bella. Before getting out on Queen Charlotte Sound the motor slowed down again and we landed and taxied to a logging camp for the night. The next day the motor ran all right, throttled back, so we crossed Queen Charlotte Sound and landed at Wadham's for gas. Here they gave us a lunch to carry with us.

We then took off for Ocean Falls but had to land, as the motor slowed up. We taxied around a little, then tried it again and stayed in the air. (We headed for Ocean Falls because we were short of money and I thought I might know someone there who would cash a check for me). Our chart was worn where it showed the entrance to the inlet at Ocean Falls so we missed the place.

Flying back toward the mountains the engine started to overheat and we landed and pulled up to a tiny beach. We were mighty glad to hear the splashing of a waterfall, which meant fresh water for the radiator. It was midnight when we again took to the air.

We sighted a boat and landed half a mile from her. As we started to taxi up to her, we ran out of gas. We lighted two distress signals, but the boat merely put her searchlight on us and went her own way! It was a tug with a raft of logs in tow—I suppose the crew couldn't afford to let go of the raft and could not tow the logs over to us. We had a few gallons of gas left in a separate can, so we filtered some into the tank in a hurry and tried to catch the boat. Just as we caught sight of her around a bend in the inlet, this gas gave out. Then we drifted until 3 a.m., when we managed to guide the plane ashore.

You may imagine we were glad of our lunch. After eating, we tried to get a little sleep in the ship. At five, after putting the last bit of our gas in the tank, we started for the mouth of the inlet. We found a lumber camp and replenished our gas supply. We discovered one of the motor braces had broken, but we thought she would fly without

The Aeromarine 40B flying boat sits tied up at Thomas Basin, southeast of the boat harbor in Ketchikan, Alaska, in July 1926. Roy Davis and Russel Merrill arrived at Ketchikan in the craft earlier that month on a flight from Vancouver, British Columbia.

it and she did! We flew to Ocean Falls, arriving there for breakfast.

At Ocean Falls we took a bath. That was an event! Then we fixed the motor brace, slept an hour, and then proceeded to Butedale with the motor working very well; averaged more than 70 miles an hour. July 4th we spent most of the day working on the motor in a pouring rain. We finally started it, but she let us down again, and we had to return.

The following day we changed all the spark plugs, and I tested her alone for 20 minutes. As she ran all right, we proceeded to Claxton, where we refueled; then we took off and flew to Ketchikan against some head wind. People seemed relieved that we had arrived, and we were certainly glad to get there.

The Navy Aerial Surveyors are here and have been cordial, offering assistance when we overhaul the motor. We beached the flying boat near a dairy and we have to keep a careful watch; the fabric on one of the wings of a Navy plane there was partially eaten by some hungry cows!

Concerned friends in Seward had wired Vancouver when the projected two-day flight stretched past a week, and the Mounties dispatched an aircraft hours before Merrill and Davis were reported safe in Ketchikan.

The next week they were unable to fly due to heavy rains. But as usual Merrill was upbeat. "Passengers, plane and weather finally all got together for ten minutes," he wrote, "and we took in ten dollars."

It was now too late in the season for Merrill and Davis to honor their cannery contracts. In Ketchikan, their only revenue-producing flying consisted of barnstorming and a series of exploratory flights for a civil engineering firm looking for hydropower sources for two cannery projects.

Although they remained in Ketchikan until early October, the two men

WE BEACHED THE FLYING BOAT NEAR A DAIRY AND WE HAVE TO KEEP A CAREFUL WATCH; THE FABRIC ON ONE OF THE WINGS OF A NAVY PLANE THERE WAS PARTIALLY EATEN BY SOME HUNGRY COWS!

— LETTER FROM RUSSEL MERRILL, DESCRIBING THE CONCLUSION OF HIS FLIGHT UP THE BRITISH COLUMBIA COAST TO ALASKA IN 1926 decided on an amicable end to their partnership. Merrill kept the Aeromarine and its spare motor. The ownership of the damaged Oriole, left in Portland, was divided equally between them. Davis returned to Portland (where he founded a flying and aircraft-maintenance school and at one point manufactured cabin monoplanes for commercial use). The Aeromarine was put into storage in Ketchikan, ending their flying for 1926.

By late September 1926, Merrill was weighing at least two solid offers to fly. The higher-salaried of the two was a personal invitation from the president of the newly formed Pacific Air Transport Company in the States. Vern C. Gorst regarded Merrill highly, having helped him secure the license that made him one of the first 118 pilots qualified to fly the mail in the United States. Within five years, Pacific Air Transport would become part of United Air Lines, the first transcontinental air transport operation.

That month Merrill also heard from Gus Gelles, the grocery wholesaler whose new oxfords and suit had withstood the rigors of his flying expedition to Kodiak with Merrill almost a year before. Gelles wired Merrill in Ketchikan to offer him the chief pilot's position with an air transport company he was helping to put together in Anchorage.

Within weeks A. A. Shonbeck, the Anchorage dealer for Caterpillar heavy construction equipment and Ford automobiles, was chosen as president and general manager of the new company, which was named Anchorage Air Transport, Inc. (AAT). Gelles became treasurer.

They hired Alonzo Cope, a mechanic with the Alaska Railroad, to organize the operational end. Cope, a big, hearty, likable man, left Anchorage October 19 by boat for the States to buy airplanes. Merrill met him two days later in Ketchikan. During the boat's layover they discussed the company and which airplanes to buy. Cope then continued his journey, which would end in Wichita, Kansas. Russel, Thyra, and the boys returned to Portland.

After considering the job offers, Merrill decided that he wanted to fly in Alaska and that the people who would do the most for aviation there would be the ones who lived and made their livelihood in that land. He had so much confidence in the future of Alaskan flying that he was willing to take a chance on the success of this Anchorage enterprise. Although he still considered Seward an ideal base, he realized Anchorage people had formed the company and he believed that city was close enough to handle business to the west. Merrill's only request was for a salary of $350 a month.

"Guess you know that I'd rather fly in Alaska and live on beans," Merrill wrote Gelles from the Pacific Northwest, "than fly down here and own a Rolls Royce."

Alonzo Cope corresponded that fall and winter with Merrill as he surveyed the commercial airplane market. Cope finally chose two products of the leading civil aircraft manufacturer of the time, the Wichita-based Travel Air Manufacturing Company.

In 1926, year-old Travel Air was on its way to becoming the world's largest producer of commercial aircraft. The company had numbered among its employees such future titans of general aviation as Walter Beech, president, and Lloyd Stearman, who had recently left his chief engineer's position at Travel Air to found his own company. Stearman left behind an engineering staff that included Ted Wells, who designed the early Beechcraft classics. Clyde Cessna was the financial brain behind the company. Anyone looking for airline equipment in 1926 made the Travel Air factory an early stop.

When Cope arrived at Travel Air in late autumn, he saw two planes that were exactly what Anchorage Air Transport needed. Both were biplanes with

THE TRAVEL AIR'S BEST FEATURE FOR NORTHERN FLYING WAS ITS ENGINE. THE PLANES WERE POWERED BY 200-HORSEPOWER WRIGHT WHIRLWIND AIR-COOLED RADIALS SIMILAR TO THE ONE THAT TOOK CHARLES LINDBERGH FROM NEW YORK TO PARIS IN 1927 "WITHOUT MISSING A BEAT," IN LINDBERGH'S WORDS.

Alonzo Cope (left) of Anchorage Air Transport Company takes delivery of two new Travel Air biplanes at the factory in Wichita, Kansas, in 1926, from Travel Air agent Jack Laass (center) and Travel Air president Walter Beech. The plane shown is the Model CW that became the air transport company's *Anchorage No. 1.*

the handsome look of every aircraft designed by Stearman, a trained architect. The Travel Airs would be the first new and fully up-to-date airplanes Russel Merrill had ever flown.

The first airplane was an open-cockpit, closed-cabin five-seat ship. Four passengers could be carried in the cabin, enclosed by the forward fuselage, while the pilot sat outdoors in an open cockpit above and behind. This type of aircraft was designated by Travel Air as Model CW. Only four were ever built.

The second was a smaller, four-seat ship with two open compartments, a Travel Air Model BW (modified). The front compartment carried two passengers side-by-side, while the after cockpit had been modified to locate the pilot's controls to the right and leave space for an additional passenger alongside. This arrangement made the rear cockpit a snug fit for two, especially with the heavy clothing required for year-round flying in Alaska, and later in use it seldom was occupied by anyone other than the pilot.

The Travel Air's best feature for northern flying was its engine. Both planes were powered by 200-horsepower Wright Whirlwind air-cooled radials similar to the one that took Charles Lindbergh from New York to Paris in 1927 "without missing a beat," in Lindbergh's words. No more water

pipes and radiators to leak or freeze up; their weight could now be carried in payload. Both planes were equipped with alternative landing gear, both wheels and skis. The smaller plane also had custom-built pontoons.

The smaller ship attained 142 miles per hour during factory testing at Wichita, which was fast for any plane then. Cope oversaw the building of the two aircraft and assembled their equipment at the factory. The two planes would be the best commercial aircraft in Alaska.

Anchorage Air Transport took great care to have the most modern and reliable accessories available, insisting upon the best of everything, almost irrespective of cost. They paid special attention to stocking such spare parts as magnetos and carburetor jets, landing gear components, and patching

Anchorage Air Transport Company's new planes are shown at Wichita, Kansas, in 1926. At right is Jack Laass with the Travel Air Model CW that became *Anchorage No. 1*; it has a four-passenger closed cabin with an open cockpit behind. At left is Alonzo Cope with the Travel Air Model BW that became *Anchorage No. 2*; it has an open two-passenger compartment with an open cockpit behind. Both planes were powered by 200-horsepower Whirlwind radial engines.

materials essential for fabric-skinned aircraft.

Anchorage Air contacted hangar builders, but it made sense to postpone construction of the hangars until summer. They investigated beacon lights, by no means universal in 1927, for the Anchorage airfield. Parachutes were considered, but the company decided they would be impractical in Alaska because they would have to be returned to the factory in the States periodically for repacking, and shipping at that time took several weeks and was undependable.

The personnel at AAT were first class. Ed Young would be the company's second pilot. Merrill recommended the Detroit-born Young for several reasons. He had military flight training with the U.S. Army Air Service at March Field, California. His earlier experience flying out of Fairbanks would be an asset. Just as important was his ground-level knowledge of the country gained while trapping on and off in Alaska and working for the Alaska Road Commission, the agency responsible not only for building roads but also for locating airfields and awarding air mail contracts. Young was an astute choice.

The formation of Anchorage Air Transport took Alaska aviation a giant step into the future. For Russel Merrill, who had spent 1926 flying a contraption that all too often took half a day to get off the water, the prospect of flying the latest commercial planes equipped with the first truly reliable engines was his own seventh heaven. He couldn't wait to get started. In February 1927, the Merrills were again bound for Alaska.

RUSSEL MERRILL WAS NOT THE ONLY AVIATOR ABOARD THE S.S. *ALASKA* WHEN IT STEAMED OUT OF SEATTLE FEBRUARY 12, 1927, ON ITS WEEKLONG VOYAGE THROUGH THE SCENIC INSIDE PASSAGE TO SEWARD. CAPTAIN HUBERT WILKINS AND HIS PARTY, INCLUDING BEN EIELSON, WERE ABOARD EN ROUTE TO WILKINS' SECOND ARCTIC EXPEDITION.

The meeting of Merrill and Eielson was electric, and they became friends immediately. A little less than three years separated them in age, with Merrill's seniority in life and superior navigational skills complemented by Eielson's greater experience and wider fame as an aviator.

Eielson's easy social graces and eagerness to live every minute to the full drew people to him. The thinning hair atop his high brow gave him the appearance of being older than he was and inspired Alaskans to call him The Professor. At once a man of books and of action, Eielson was the more talkative of the two.

Each pilot had something to learn from the other. No contemporary pilot had Eielson's background in different aircraft types over terrain from Florida to the Arctic Ocean.

Eielson had won his wings with the U.S. Army Air Service and, like Merrill, was a college man. He had come to Alaska to teach school at Fairbanks, meanwhile hoping to get back into flying. In 1923 he talked two Fairbanks businessmen into putting up $1,000 for a Curtiss Jenny, with which he made the first commercial airplane flight in that city.

The following year, after Eielson flew an experimental air mail route from Fairbanks to McGrath eight times (of the contracted ten), the Post Office recalled the DH-4BM aircraft they had provided on loan. Eielson had

Overleaf: Russel Merrill preparing to go on a flight in the Travel Air open passenger cockpit BW airplane from Anchorage in the winter.

used up all the spare parts that had accompanied the plane, repairing it after each of several unfortunate landing incidents on Weeks Field.

Eielson bounced around outside Alaska before being recruited to join the Wilkins expedition to explore the arctic polar ice cap in 1926. Now Eielson and Wilkins were returning for a second year. Their 1926 season had been almost as disappointing as Merrill's. They had abandoned their efforts after flying three round trips to Barrow in the single-engine Fokker *Alaskan* plus flying another 1,200 miles in the trimotor Fokker *Detroiter*.

The plan for 1927 for the Detroit News-Wilkins Arctic Expedition was to use their base at Barrow, the northernmost settlement in the United States, to make flights over the Arctic Ocean. Wilkins, a 38-year-old Australian, was already famous after walking most of the arctic coast with Vilhjalmur Stefannson's Canadian Arctic Expedition, which discovered several of the world's last major land masses between 1913 and 1917, and serving as the naturalist in Ernest Shackleton's Antarctic expedition in 1921 and 1922.

Surviving explorations near both poles to become an old man, Wilkins later wrote in his memoir *Flying in the Arctic* that Eielson "was a ready, deliberate, reasoning pilot. He met emergencies calmly. . . . He summed up every situation and looked at it from all angles and then, whenever there was a chance, he went ahead." They were a good team. Whereas Eielson was weak on navigation skills, Wilkins was a trained navigator.

During the voyage north, Wilkins outlined his dream of flying over the North Pole. He said that though they hadn't made it last year, they would sometime. But, he told the Merrills, that was not his main objective.

Wilkins was dedicated to establishing beyond doubt the existence of land between Alaska and the North Pole. Wilkins also wanted to interest the circumpolar nations in establishing meteorological stations in the higher latitudes and using the data for forecasting weather around the globe.

Another goal was to search for a commercial air route across the top of the world. In spite of the airship *Norge*'s flight over the North Pole in 1926, Wilkins believed that the airplane, not the dirigible, was the most suitable transportation in the Arctic. If he and Eielson could make the first trans-Arctic nonstop flight, their success would go a long way toward proving Wilkins' theories.

With their relatively close Southcentral Alaska locations, Anchorage and Fairbanks were natural rivals to become the hub of trans-Arctic flights to Asia and Europe and of aerial activity within the Territory of Alaska.

Up to 1927, as documented in Robert Stevens' *Alaskan Aviation History,* much more activity had taken place in Fairbanks. As early as 1913, James Martin had made five flights there in an aircraft of his own design. Eielson flew out of Fairbanks for three months in each of 1923 and 1924. Permanent operations by Alaska Aerial Transportation Company and others started in 1924.

Anchorage got its start in aviation in 1922, with Charles Hammontree flying a Boeing C-11S floatplane that had been shipped in and assembled there. Roy Troxel crashed the same Boeing plane beyond repair on his first takeoff in 1924. Noel Wien assembled, tested, and barnstormed a Hisso-powered Standard J-1 at Anchorage for eighteen days in 1924 for Alaska Aerial Transportation before delivering it to its base in Fairbanks. Merrill had flown his Curtiss F-boat into Anchorage for a week in 1925. In 1926, no one had flown at Anchorage.

Now it was 1927 and the Merrill family and the members of the Wilkins Expedition shared an anticipation so intense that conversations among them barely paused when the *Alaska* docked at Seward. The next morning, February 20, they boarded the train for the last leg of their journey. Eielson joined them once again, and the voyagers settled back to enjoy the coming hours.

When the conductor arrived to collect tickets, Eielson rose to his feet and warmly shook hands with the man. Eielson then turned and introduced the Merrills to the one-and-only Jimmy Rodebaugh.

After the conductor moved on, Eielson explained that Rodebaugh was head of the Bennett-Rodebaugh Company in Fairbanks. Rodebaugh wore many hats: he had made a good grubstake out of fur trading as well as being senior conductor on the Alaska Railroad. Rodebaugh was bitten by the flying bug a couple of years before, Eielson said. Rodebaugh went to San Diego to learn to fly, then ordered a couple of J-1 Standards and brought in a pilot, Noel Wien, to fly for him. Nevertheless, Rodebaugh, a practical man, had kept his day job.

The train pulled in to the little station at Anchorage, and Russel and Thyra said a heartfelt goodbye to Wilkins and Eielson, who were continuing on to Fairbanks. The group passed around best wishes for success in all of their undertakings.

This is Anchorage as it looked in the 1920s. The airfield is the snow-covered area to the right in the photo, at the edge of town between Ninth and Tenth streets (now called Ninth and Tenth avenues).

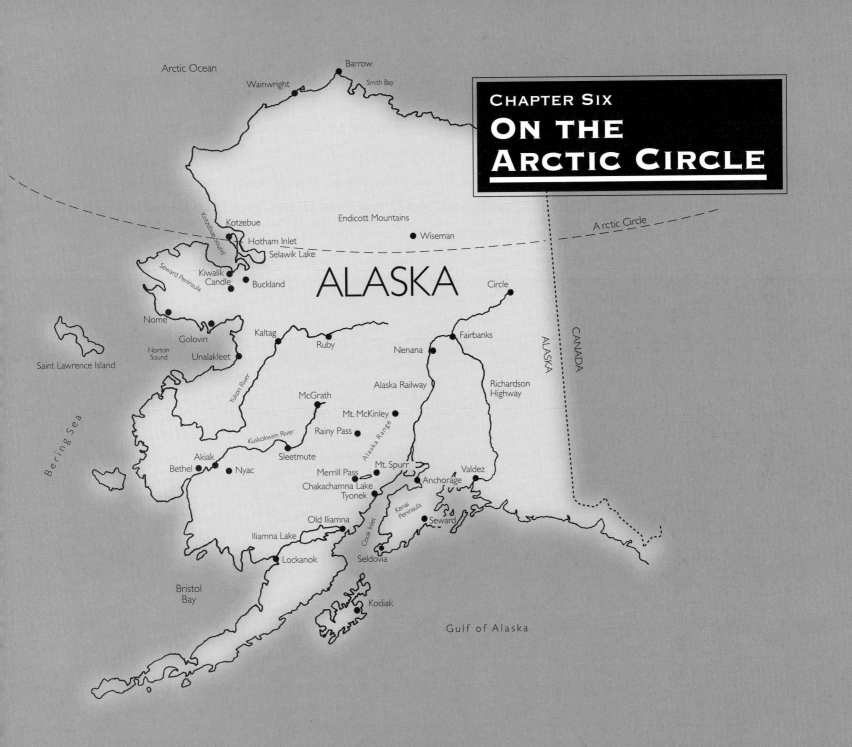

Arctic Ocean

Barrow

Wainwright

Smith Bay

Kotzebue Sound

Kotzebue

Endicott Mountains

Wiseman

Arctic Circle

Hotham Inlet

Selawik Lake

Seward Peninsula

Kiwalik

Candle

Buckland

ALASKA

Circle

ALASKA

CANADA

Nome

Golovin

Norton Sound

Kaltag

Ruby

Fairbanks

Saint Lawrence Island

Unalakleet

Nenana

Alaska Railway

Richardson Highway

Yukon River

McGrath

Mt. McKinley

Bering Sea

Kuskokwim River

Rainy Pass

Alaska Range

Akiak

Sleetmute

Bethel

Nyac

Merrill Pass

Mt. Spurr

Valdez

Chakachamna Lake

Tyonek

Anchorage

Old Iliamna

Kenai Peninsula

Seward

Iliamna Lake

Cook Inlet

Seldovia

Lockanok

Bristol Bay

Kodiak

Gulf of Alaska

THE MERRILLS SOON FOUND A LITTLE THREE-ROOM FRAME HOUSE AT FIFTH AVENUE AND L STREET, FOUR BLOCKS FROM THE AIRFIELD AT ANCHORAGE. THE AVIATION FIELD, AS ALONZO COPE CALLED IT, WAS ON THE OUTSKIRTS OF THE CITY, BETWEEN NINTH AND TENTH STREETS. THE CITY HAD CLEARED IT IN 1923 AND DESIGNATED IT AS THE MUNICIPAL AIRFIELD. EVEN WITH THIS OFFICIAL STATUS, ITS SAFETY HAZARDS WOULD MAKE MODERN AVIATORS SHUDDER: A ROAD RAN ACROSS THE FIELD, AND A LINE OF TALL TREES AND TELEPHONE WIRES BORDERED THE LANDING STRIP.

Anchorage had mushroomed during construction of the Alaska Railroad, which began in 1915. Instead of stagnating like so many northern boomtowns, Anchorage continued to modernize, paving its streets, lighting them, and lining them with modern shops and services.

The Merrills found their fellow townspeople as cordial as the residents of southeastern Alaska had been. It was a social town: besides five churches and four fraternal orders, Anchorage boasted no fewer than eleven billiard and pool halls. While Russel threw himself into his work with Anchorage Air Transport, Thyra soon learned why Anchorage was known as the City of Hospitality.

Thyra remembered those first weeks in Anchorage in detail:

When I am asked "Did you have to endure any hardships in Alaska?" my answer is that old cliche "Yes—and no."

I never lived in the backwoods, away from the necessities and conveniences of a civilized life. I was surrounded by understanding friends, I had my own furniture, and the comforts of a normal city life. I could buy the latest-style clothing in the Anchorage shops. There was medical attention at hand, and I could go to a movie or a dance when and if I felt inclined. Roughing it was a game confined to duck hunting around Cook Inlet or a week in the cabins at McKinley Park.

But I was subjected to hardships, the tension and suspense that accompanied my husband's flying activities. While we were still getting settled in

The Anchorage Municipal Airfield in 1927, commonly called "the park strip," was crossed by a public road (foreground), I Street.

the house, I slipped on the ice and broke my ankle. I was rushed to the hospital. The bone was badly splintered, and a heavy cast was put on. The hospital was full, and I had to be moved home the second day.

While I was getting used to crutches, I found by experimenting that I could rest my knee above the cast on a chair, push it in front of me, and, at the same time, hop with the other foot. So I propelled myself awkwardly about the house and took up aban-

doned duties. There were hot fires to be kept up in the coal range and in the furnace.

There was, however, a compensation for each difficult day. My front windows looked out on the Inlet, and the children and I could watch the breathtaking drama that nature enacted to the west. The sun made a definite path of brilliant orange light. The frozen ice was broken up by the moving of the tide, each berg taking on new color effects as it slowly shifted. Mount Susitna was a hazy, ethereal mauve, but the Alaska Range beyond remained a startling white. Sunset always left me with a sense of peace and an inner conviction that Russel was all right.

The pair of Travel Air biplanes arrived in Anchorage on March 1, 1927. The shipment from Wichita was shepherded north by Alonzo Cope and Travel Air factory representative Jack Laass. Laass had flown a Travel Air powered by a Wright J-4 in the previous year's Ford Reliability Tour—an event that was a milestone in proving that aircraft are capable of routine flights on schedule.

The Anchorage Air Transport planes were shipped in eleven crates. Anchorage had a heavy snowfall that winter, and two feet of snow still covered the airfield. Alternating thaws and cold spells had created layers of soft snow and hard-packed, frozen snow. The company had decided to delay construction of a hangar until later in the year, so the crates were hauled on horse-drawn sleds to Oscar Gill's Garage, five blocks from the airfield.

The smaller plane, designated *Anchorage No. 2,* arrived with Department of Commerce number C-193 painted in white on its fin and rudder. This plane, with its open passenger compartment and open cockpit behind, was the first of the two aircraft to be put together. Everything but the wings was assembled within the tight confines of the garage.

They mounted the plane on skis. The use of skis on aircraft had not yet been perfected in Alaska, so Alonzo Cope had bought a pair of Seversky all-metal skis to experiment with. Long, narrow, and light, they were popular on the East Coast and in Canada.

Outside Gill's the temperature was 8 degrees Fahrenheit below zero, with a bone-chilling wind. Because of the weather, it took two days to assemble and attach No. 2's biplane wings, with their struts and crisscrossed bracing wires.

The air-cooled Whirlwind motor was the latest word in power-plant technology. But it was new to Alaska and difficult to start and warm up in the extreme cold. Its fuel system had been set to run in Kansas, where very small carburetor jets were used for economy. The miserly factory settings didn't work, so the fuel-air mixture in the carburetor had to be enriched.

To help start the engine, they hung a canvas shroud over and around the motor and operated an oil stove under it—a technique that became the time-honored method of starting air-cooled radial engines in the far north. To maintain the engine's minimum operating temperature, they devised a metal cowling to cover the crankcase and the lower halves of the exposed cylinders, wrapping it partway around each.

Once the Whirlwind was started, it would only turn up to 1,000 rpm, becoming unsteady and eventually cutting out above that level. It took two days to diagnose the trouble: the cowling was drawing current from the high-tension wires, which were insufficiently insulated. New ignition wires cured the problem.

Anchorage No. 2 was now ready to fly. Jack Laass taxied it to the airstrip on March 7 and took it up for a test flight. The plane checked out fine, but

TO HELP START THE ENGINE, THEY HUNG A CANVAS SHROUD OVER AND AROUND THE MOTOR AND OPERATED AN OIL STOVE UNDER IT—A TECHNIQUE THAT BECAME THE TIME-HONORED METHOD OF STARTING AIR-COOLED RADIAL ENGINES IN THE FAR NORTH.

Anchorage Air Transport Company flew two Travel Air biplanes: the Model BW (foreground), named *Anchorage No. 2*, and the larger Model CW, *Anchorage No. 1*, which featured a four-passenger cabin. The planes are shown here at Anchorage in 1927.

on landing the thin skis broke through two of the three crusts of snow. The left ski turned under and broke at the axle. The axle and then the left wingtip caught in the snow and the ship stood on its nose, breaking the propeller. The left lower wing spar and the adjacent longeron were bent at the landing gear.

All this damage added up to a hard lesson about northern aviation: narrow skis are only good on hard ice. The oil was drained from the motor, and the next morning the plane was hauled back to Gill's Garage. Merrill, Cope, and Laass began rebuilding the left wing, enlarging the carburetor jets, installing a new walnut Hartzell propeller, and fitting on new skis.

Anchorage No. 1, the cabin plane with the open cockpit behind, was assembled while No. 2 was being repaired. The bigger aircraft was shod with a pair of wooden skis purchased from National Air Transport in Kansas City. Ed Young, Anchorage Air Transport's second pilot, tested the cabin plane. It checked out fine. On March 10 Young flew *Anchorage No. 1* northwest to McGrath, then southwest to Bethel, two towns on the Kuskokwim River, flying a total of 515 miles.

Young hit very cold weather on the trip, overcowled the engine, and melted the tops of three pistons. With No. 2 still undergoing repairs, AAT arranged to have the Bennett-Rodebaugh Company of Fairbanks deliver parts to Young, who had gone down twenty miles from Bethel. The Fairbanks airline was co-owned by Jimmy Rodebaugh, the Alaska Railroad conductor Merrill had been introduced to only a couple of weeks before.

By March 15, No. 2 was ready to fly again. Merrill tested it this time and became familiar with the aircraft, which was faster and more modern than any he had flown. Four days later he set out to take the fur-buying Wandling brothers to Iliamna Lake. But on takeoff, the aircraft's left ski hit a chunk of

AND SO AFTER TWELVE DAYS OF OPERATION, THE ANCHORAGE AIR TRANSPORT COMPANY HAD BOTH ITS AIRPLANES GROUNDED FOR REPAIRS, ONE OF THEM IN THE WILD KUSKOKWIM COUNTRY.

ice. The plane ground-looped and came to rest on its right wing. No one was injured, and on March 20th, the ever-faithful horses again dragged the sled and *Anchorage No. 2* back to the garage.

Gill's was too small to handle work simultaneously on both the fuselage and wings of the damaged aircraft, so the work was divided between Gill's and the carpentry shop of the Alaska Railroad. At the shop Laass and Charlie Bisel, a patternmaker with the railroad, repaired the spruce wing ribs and spars while the rest of the AAT crew worked on the fuselage uptown at the garage.

And so after twelve days of operation, the company had both its airplanes grounded, one of them in the wild Kuskokwim River country. The company had already used up its supply of wing fabric and dope, so Bennett-Rodebaugh loaned a stock of the materials—but it still was not enough to cover all of No. 2's wing surfaces. Laass and Bisel resorted to using bed sheets instead of aircraft-quality fabric and mixed their own dope from banana oil and glue.

Four days later, before No. 2 was reassembled, the versatile Jack Laass was called back to the States. With Young rebuilding his engine in the Kuskokwim, Laass gone, and Thyra hobbled by her broken ankle, Merrill had his hands full. He and Cope now constituted the entire crew of Anchorage Air Transport.

Merrill's reward came March 30 when, with No. 2 back together, he was finally able to take off once again in the fastest, sweetest-handling ship he had ever flown. He made several short flights around Anchorage, liking the Travel Air more each day. He was back in his element.

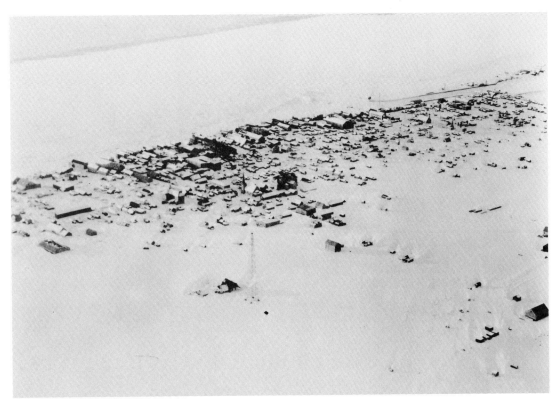

Nome sits in its world of snow in the winter of 1928. Planes landed on the ice in front of town (top of picture). Residents of Nome and of Candle backed the Anchorage Air Transport operation by subscribing to company stock.

On April 5, 1927, Merrill and Cope found themselves in Nome with the Travel Air No. 2 warmed up and nowhere to go. They had flown there as volunteers in answer to a wired appeal to airlift a dying man from St. Lawrence Island, 160 miles to the southwest in the Bering Sea, to the hospital at Nome. They were more than willing to attempt the first-ever flight to the island; if anything, they looked forward to pioneering the route. But with the 9 a.m. weather report from the island came the news that the man had died overnight.

They were considering barnstorming around Nome until a fellow guest at their hotel asked Merrill to fly him to Candle, some 150 miles northeast of Nome across the Seward Peninsula. The passenger was Hilkey Robinson, a fur buyer and proprietor of a store in Candle. He wanted to know why Anchorage Air Transport didn't fly this territory; only a few airplanes had ever been in the area. Merrill said AAT didn't provide service because of the peninsula's severe weather. But AAT was out to find business, and if it was warranted, the company would certainly fly there.

What started as a marginally paying flight to remote Candle became a highly profitable proposition when Edgar Broadway, a mining engineer with the Hammond Consolidated Gold Fields of Nome, decided to fly the round trip to Candle just to see the country from the air. In addition an attorney arranged to be picked up on the return trip from Nome to Anchorage.

By the time Merrill took off with Broadway, Robinson, and Robinson's load of furs and luggage, there was no room for Cope in No. 2, the two-cockpit open plane. Merrill left Cope with his charted course, just in case of trouble. Merrill described the difficulties of the trip—and sudden disaster—in a letter:

When we took off for Candle it was pretty cloudy. We had received a report of clear weather down the coast, and another from Kotzebue Sound beyond Candle stating that it was clear but that there was a strong wind. I didn't feel much like going because the weather at Nome was not what it should have been.

But I thought I was foolish not to go in view of the favorable reports from surrounding districts, especially as we had such fine weather all the way from Anchorage to within a short distance of Nome. So we took off at about 2 p.m., expecting to be back the same evening. We went along the coast under low clouds until we found a good-sized hole. I went up through

The open-passenger-cockpit *Anchorage No. 2* is seen just after flying into the ice in a blizzard at Selawik Lake on the Arctic Circle on April 5, 1927. Russel Merrill and his two passengers escaped serious injury.

this to look the country over and found it was reasonably clear in the direction we were going.

I went for an hour on what I thought was the correct course, but couldn't see the Arctic Ocean, as I expected to in that length of time. I landed on a river and asked my passengers if they knew where they were. It was rather thick so we couldn't see far. Neither of them knew, but one said that he could tell as soon as we came out to open, or rather frozen, water. We took off, and in about ten minutes we came to a reindeer corral; I flew low to get a good look at it. However, the others did not recognize the place.

I proceeded, thinking we would soon find something that my Candle passenger would recognize. In the next fifteen minutes we saw nothing that was familiar to him.

I was about to turn back to the corral when, without warning, we were caught in a blinding snowstorm. At first I didn't realize that it was snow, but thought it was the clouds coming closer over the ground or ice. Although my altimeter read over 300 feet, I realized, of course, that wasn't our actual altitude, since the altimeter reads from sea level. I took a chance and came down a little to try to see under the haze.

Before I knew it we struck the ice at full speed and turned over! As we climbed out, the ice was swept clear for an instant and we saw a track fully three inches deep that the tail skid had gouged for more than 100 yards.

They had been flying on the ground without knowing it! The plane struck an ice hummock that flipped the aircraft on its back. Later, in a cable from Nome to the Associated Press, Hilkey Robinson continued the story:

We crawled out and discovered we were in a real old-time blizzard, the kind I hadn't seen for fifteen years. The plane was damaged. We were all slightly bruised and made haste to shelter ourselves from the freezing weather, using the plane body and part of the wings as a windbreak.

We spent two nights and a day without bedding and with very little fire. We had to keep awake all of the time, or we would have frozen. We used pieces of the wings and skis as fuel to heat water.

On the second day, the shoreline became visible. We made for a bunch of willows ahead, thinking we were in Buckland Bay. But, not finding any cabins there, we were forced to wait for clear weather until we could sight

landmarks. At 2 p.m. we caught sight of a range of mountains that we recognized and located our whereabouts to be on Selawik Lake, about five miles from Hotham Inlet. We were exactly on the Arctic Circle!

We started for Callahan's shelter cabin and stayed out in the open that night. At 8:30 the next morning, just after we had reached shelter at the cabin, another storm came up.

That evening, two natives with dog teams arrived from Noorvik. They gave us some schee, a fish similar to whitefish, and some rabbit, which was very welcome after our diet of rice. We engaged the natives to take us to

The wreckage of *Anchorage No. 2* lies on the ice at Selawik Lake after a day and a half in a snowstorm. Parts of the wings had been cut off and set on the fuselage to make a shelter for Russel Merrill and his two passengers following the April 5, 1927, crash.

Candle, and we arrived there at 10:45 p.m. April 9, after traveling all day in the storm.

As to hardships encountered, we leave that to the imagination of old-timers who have weathered real storms in the open. Outside of my broken nose and a few bruises, we're all OK, but rather fatigued. The pilot and Mr. Broadway were efficient and rapid thinkers, and good companions in their first Arctic experience.

Our present wish is that we would like to make another flight with Mr. Merrill. All Candle is delighted with our safety, but disappointed at being cheated out of the thrill they were expecting. Summing it all up, outside of bad weather encountered, my enthusiasm about flying is not dampened in the least. I feel that the way of distant travel by dog team is doomed.

The following day, April 10, Merrill wired AAT and Thyra to let them know he was safe. Then he arranged with H. W. Johnston of the Lomen Reindeer and Trading Company to retrieve the airplane with dogs or reindeer. Merrill was planning to leave Candle the next day, but was instructed by wire to remain there, pending instructions by AAT's president, A. A. Shonbeck.

A frustrating week went by before Merrill got a wire from Anchorage, asking the cost of moving the plane. Since H. W. Johnston, the man who would do the job, was away in the village of Buckland, east of Candle, Merrill wired back an estimate of $200 or less to get the plane to Candle.

Johnston arrived in Candle April 20, urging Merrill to get on with the job of retrieving the plane. In his handwritten log, Merrill noted that Johnston "had reindeer brought to Buckland for our use but sent them back as he couldn't hold the herdsmen. Bears attack the herds this time of year. He stated the lakes and especially the rivers were due to overflow the ice in ten days or so, so if we did not start for the plane shortly he could not help us. Wired Anchorage stating there was a danger of overflow and would start for plane early tomorrow morning. . . . Bought parka, fur pants, gloves, sun glasses, underwear, and did washing."

On April 21 Merrill mushed to Buckland with Johnston. Merrill's logbook tells the story of the grueling retrieval operation:

The damaged fuselage of *Anchorage No. 2* is mounted on sleds for the trip from Selawik Lake to Candle. Identification of the two men is uncertain, but they probably are the dog team musher H. W. Johnston and his helper.

April 22—Came to Igloo Point and outfitted there. Using 11 Johnston's dogs and 8 Robinson's. One native, Harry, also taken. Started from Buckland at 5:56 a.m., drove to 5:00 p.m. (stopped one and a half hours at Igloo Point). Started to blow ground snow one hour out of Igloo Point, regular blizzard at start of Portage and from there to Hotham Inlet. It was good weather at Igloo Point—could see land on all sides of Buckland Bay. Made camp along shore of Hotham Inlet, very stormy. Had some of Amundsen's milk chocolate—excellent.

The parts of *Anchorage No. 2* are hauled by dog teams from Selawik Lake to Candle. The fuselage is in the foreground; a second dog team, pulling sleds holding the wings, is in the background.

(This was from a small cache made by the Arctic explorer Roald Amundsen on one of his expeditions.)

April 23—Too stormy to travel, visibility about one mile. Dried out clothing.

April 24—Stormy but visibility about one mile. Went to plane in morning and prepared it for trip. One ski placed across landing gear and two deer sleds under that. One dogsled was put under tail skid.

April 25—Took all 19 dogs to start [moving] fuselage and get to open snow. Later used 11 dogs on fuselage and 8 on dogsled with wings and supplies. Load too heavy for dogs even though all three men walked. It was poor snow for sledding, about two feet loose snow on top. Made about 15 miles to place on Hotham Inlet where we camped before.

April 26—On trail by 6 a.m. but took until afternoon to make 6 miles to Callahan's cabin. Used all dogs on fuselage on north side of portage. Had to go back for wings, etc. Dogs pretty tired. Decided to rest remainder of day and go direct to Kiwalik instead of attempting to make Chovis Peninsula. That night Johnston and Harry partially snow blind.

April 27—Made straight for Kiwalik but could not make it so made camp in open overnight. On trail 6 a.m. to 5 p.m. Snow loose for about two feet and hard going. Johnston and Harry now badly snow blind. Johnston led his dogs all the way, had practically lost his voice urging dogs.

April 28—On trail 5:45, made Kiwalik [less than ten miles north of Candle] at 1 p.m. Hard going. Phoned Candle and found Ed Young and Cope there with the big ship [the company's other plane, Anchorage No. 1].

Merrill, Cope, and Young spent the next three days dismantling and crating the motor, fuselage, and wings of the damaged airplane. The motor was loaded on dogsleds May 2 for Unalakleet, 170 miles south on Norton Sound, for the soonest-possible shipment by water to Anchorage. The wings and fuselage were left for later shipment via Kotzebue Sound after the ice there broke up.

Merrill's off-the-cuff estimate of $200 or less for pulling the Travel Air to Candle turned out to be surprisingly accurate. Johnston charged a total of $180 "including dog team, grub, and native." Robinson made no charge for his team.

The main street of Candle, Alaska, is piled high with winter snow. Two Alaskans with dog teams brought Russel Merrill and his two passengers to Candle after he crash-landed April 5, 1927, at Selawik Lake.

At Candle, the men of Anchorage Air Transport made plans for their flight back to Anchorage. Alonzo Cope tells the story:

Monday morning we loaded the motor on the dogsleds and saw the dogs start to Unalakleet. Then we gathered up the mail and a few things the people in Candle wanted to send to Nome. The mail was going to Nome only in the summertime. There was no winter mail to Candle, so everybody had a package or a postcard or something to send to friends in Nome or back in the States. We had the ship loaded and all Merrill and I could do was to get into the cabin. Ed was flying.

Even at that we couldn't take all that the people wanted us to take—there would have been two cabins full. Then too, we wouldn't have been able to haul it on account of the small field in Candle. We had landed, and [were] taking off, from a small bar in the Kiwalik River. The river had a pressure ridge and rough ice, making it impossible to use the runway that would have been available had not this rough ice been there.

Anyway, we got in the air, Ed headed straight for Nome, and although it only took an hour and thirty minutes, he flew through three snowstorms before we reached Nome. Had we arrived in Nome twenty minutes later we couldn't have landed on account of a snowstorm.

When they arrived at Nome they found that a Dr. Rex F. Swartz had arranged for Anchorage Air Transport to fly a regular air service between Nome and Anchorage. Residents of Nome and Candle were backing the operation by subscribing to AAT stock. Swartz, of the Anchorage Government Hospital, had arrived in Nome with Ed Young as a representative of AAT to develop business for the company around the Seward Peninsula. Nome, the Alaskan town closest to Siberia, would now have better access to the outside world.

On May 4, *Anchorage No. 1* flew out of Nome with Ed Young in the cockpit and Merrill, Cope, Dr. Swartz, and a mountain of mail, equipment, and souvenirs in the cabin. They got only as far as Golovin, less than eighty miles east, with the weather too bad to continue.

Cope resumes his account of the flight back to Anchorage that took many times longer than expected and included a bizarre dunking in the Tanana River:

From the fourth to the ninth we stayed at Golovin, and that seemed like a month. Golovin is just a small village of about fifteen people, two white and the rest natives, and 300 malamute dogs! The malamute chorus never let up!

We were very anxious to leave the place, for it was lonesome sitting around with nothing to do; the breakup [of the winter ice on bodies of water] was coming and we didn't know just where we were going to land, having skis on the plane.

There was an old piano in the roadhouse. One day after Young, Merrill, and myself finished a game of poker, Russ got up from the table, stretched and yawned, and moved all of the years of dust, accumulated old papers, etc., from the piano, we thought for a tour of inspection. Then he sat down and played.

I don't know when anything sounded so sweet, as we had heard nothing but the dogs for so long. From then on we would make Russ play for about two hours every day. Russ complained about the piano being out of tune and hard to play, but that made no difference to us. We made him play just the same.

The morning of the ninth, the weather reports were favorable, and we took off from Golovin and aimed to fly straight to McGrath and Anchorage. But before we got to the Yukon River, we were over a solid bank of clouds, just now and then seeing a mountain peak stick through the clouds.

Russ and I had a lot of fun with Dr. S., kidding him about the safety of airplane motors. This was Dr. S.'s second ride and his first ride over the clouds. We told him that if the motor ever quit he could just count himself out. Really, it didn't look any too good to us, but we thought we would keep up the spirits somehow.

In about two hours we came over a hole in the clouds, and below us—just below us—was solid ice, signs of a river. This proved to be the Yukon

River, so instead of going by way of McGrath, we followed the Yukon River to Ruby, refueled there, took on some mail, and took off for Nenana.

We learned at Ruby that we would have to land at Nenana on the ice, the Fairbanks field having no snow on it. We landed on the Tanana River, right near the tripod that they placed out in the middle of the river to be carried away with the first movement of the ice. This was to determine the official time of the breakup at Nenana.

We landed on skis and were going to change to wheels so we could take off from there and land on the field (at Nenana), so we removed the skis and put on the wheels and started to turn the ship around to head into the wind for the takeoff. But when the ship started to move, the ice was so rotten the ship went right down through to the fuselage. It went down so fast the prop was turning in the ice before Ed could cut the switch. The ice was so rotten that it didn't even break the wooden propeller we were using.

The railroad was getting their boats ready to put into the water as soon as the ice moved out, and there were about a hundred men on the shore watching us. When they saw the ship go down with the [lower] wings on the ice, about ten men came out to help us. It was some time before they could get there as they had to put a small boat into the water to cross from the bank to the cake of ice on which we had landed.

Finally they got there and we raised the ship and put it back on its skis. After we had the ship resting safely on its skis again we thoroughly examined the ice on the river to see where there was a spot hard enough to support wheels, for there was just one thing to do and that was to take off from the ice on wheels and land on the field.

We finally found what we thought would be a good spot, up close to the railroad bridge, and moved the ship up there on its skis, and again installed the wheels on the ship.

This time we took everything out of the airplane, even the tool roll; also drained some gas out so the ship would be just as light as possible so the wheels wouldn't sink through the ice again. This time the ship succeeded in getting off, it being very light, taking only about 200 feet to lift off.

In fact, the ship was so very light Ed had to make three attempts to get into the field. He had been used to flying the ship with so much overload it was really hard to fly when it was light. . . . The ice went out [at Nenana] May 11 that year, two days after we had our scramble with the ship.

The night of the ninth Russ called Mrs. Merrill, the first time he had talked to her since the fourth of April. And Russ remarked, "Gosh, it seems good to talk to Thyra again."

The morning of the tenth we all piled in the ship and came to Anchorage. We tied the ship down out on the aviation field, and all came home to our baths and haircuts, changes of clothing, and to rest up.

Thyra had plenty of reason to reflect on her first six weeks in Anchorage. She wrote:

That month, with Russel at Candle, was a difficult time of physical and mental strain that is difficult to forget, though I learned to joke about it afterwards.

The pain in my ankle subsided, and I thought that it had knitted at last, until I realized that it was completely numb. Examination showed that I had jarred the cast, cutting off the circulation, and I was threatened with gangrene infection. For one night there was some question whether my leg could be saved.

I was grateful to be up and around again when Russel finally returned the day before Dick's birthday [May 11], and I planned a joint celebration. Wanting to demonstrate my knowledge of cooking, I made Dick's birthday cake while Russel was out at the field and set it out to cool.

While the children were taking their naps, I thought I smelled smoke, and I limped into the kitchen. A sheet of fire stretched across one wall, and in less than two minutes, just time enough for me to rouse the children and get them outside, the whole place was in flames.

I went back to the house and telephoned for the fire department. The fire was eating through the tinder-dry wood and I didn't have time to save a thing. The firemen came in a minute, but already the structure was a furnace.

When Russel arrived home shortly after, he found the smoking skeleton of a house, his wife standing in the cold in a thin housedress, and his children, clad only in their night clothes, at a neighbor's. Again, Thyra's words:

I could only be thankful that I had been able to get the children out safely, and I felt more distress for Russel, after his hard experience at Candle, than for myself. But when we finally went into the ruins, I think I felt worse about the charred cake, laid out for the festive dinner, than about my melted silver and blackened china.

Anchorage Air Transport's cabin Travel Air on Spenard Lake at Anchorage. The hoist was used for changing from pontoons to wheels and back as needed. A small dirt runway nearby allowed planes on wheels to be flown to the municipal airfield in town.

CHAPTER SEVEN

A THING OF SHREDS & PATCHES

RUSS WAS GONE SOME TWO HOURS. I WAS WORRIED PINK WONDERING WHAT HAD HAPPENED. I THOUGHT OF A MILLION THINGS THAT COULD HAVE HAPPENED.

— ALONZO COPE, WAITING FOR RUSSEL MERRILL TO RETURN FROM THE TEST FLIGHT OF THE REBUILT *ANCHORAGE NO. 1*, ON JULY 29, 1927

MERRILL FLEW THE CABIN PLANE, *ANCHORAGE NO. 1,* FOR THE FIRST TIME ON MAY 15, 1927. HE DID SOME PRACTICE FLIGHTS, THEN STARTED FLYING PASSENGERS. *ANCHORAGE NO. 1* WAS NO GREAT MYSTERY TO HIM; HE HAD, AFTER ALL, HELPED ASSEMBLE IT. AS WITH NO. 2, THOUGH, HE WAS ABOUT TO BECOME INTIMATE WITH ITS INNERMOST WORKINGS.

The Bristol Bay cannery contracts that had gone unfulfilled in 1926 beckoned again with meat-and-potatoes work. These flights required planes with pontoons because airfields were scarce but places to land on water were plentiful at the canneries. Anchorage Air Transport had pontoons for the smaller open-cockpit plane, but that craft had been damaged at Candle and was out of service. The company didn't have any pontoons designed for the heavier cabin plane now at Anchorage.

They had to make do, mounting the smaller pontoons on the larger plane. Merrill and Alonzo Cope were aware the smaller floats presented a danger because they weren't built to support the heavier plane, but the men felt they had no choice. Adapting struts and bracing wires to fit the pontoons took them three days.

With *Anchorage No. 1's* total useful load capacity down to 900 pounds, only one of the three passengers waiting in Anchorage June 19 could leave that day for the Libby, McNeil & Libby cannery at Lockanok, some 300 miles southwest of Anchorage on Bristol Bay. The three passengers and their luggage would exceed the new limit. The issue was settled when two of the men seemed relieved not to have to go first, leaving H. B. Friele of the Nakat Packing Company as Merrill's only passenger when he took off at 6 p.m.

The flight to Lockanok took three hours. (The two men who were reluctant to fly ended up walking partway and traveling by boat the rest of the distance, taking a total of five days to get to the same place.) Because it was too late in the day for an immediate return trip, Merrill moored *Anchorage No. 1* in the mouth of the Alagnak River in front of the cannery.

By the next morning a steady 70-mile-an-hour gale blew out of the northeast. Without enough fuel to buck the wind back to Anchorage, Merrill decided to wait it out. By evening the storm had quieted to intermittent gusts, but the wind was now blowing across the river. The plane, silhouetted against the gray storm and foaming whitecaps, became a plaything of the elements: as the wind lulled, the airplane would swing downstream from its mooring; as it picked up, the airplane would weather-vane its nose into the storm.

The gale let up and then quickly resumed. One sudden blast caught the airplane sideways, lifted the windward wings, and flipped *Anchorage No. 1* over on its back in the middle of the river. There the plane wallowed, upside down, with the tide coming in and gale-driven waves pounding its belly. Merrill could do nothing.

The gale was now at its height. Merrill and the cannery workers hoped that at low tide the plane would rest on the mud floor of the river. Their plan was to tie some buoys to the Travel Air and float it to shore on the incoming tide. Merrill wired AAT and requested Cope's help.

At low water the wind was blowing as hard as ever. The gale persisted for three days. Who could have expected this at the beginning of summer? They attempted to tow the cannery's pile driver and a boat to the airplane from downwind and lift No. 1 from the water, but even with their low superstructures, they were driven back to shore. Merrill spent all night aboard the pile driver, keeping an eye on his overturned plane.

THE GALE LET UP AND THEN QUICKLY RESUMED. ONE SUDDEN BLAST CAUGHT THE AIRPLANE SIDEWAYS, LIFTED THE WINDWARD WINGS, AND FLIPPED *ANCHORAGE NO. 1* OVER ON ITS BACK IN THE MIDDLE OF THE RIVER.

Anchorage No. I upside down after being turned over by the wind on June 19, 1927, while moored at Lockanok cannery off of Bristol Bay. The plane was battered by wind and waves for three days in a 70-mile-per-hour gale before it could be recovered.

When the winds subsided, the pile driver was anchored nearby and a boom was set out toward the stricken aircraft. The rescuers attached a cable to the plane's tail skid. The motorized winch gathered power, the cable went taut, No. 1's tail rose—and the upside-down airplane separated just behind the cockpit. All four fuselage longerons parted. Wires, cables, and shredded fabric were all that connected the cabin, motor, and wings to the rear fuselage and tail, held in the air by the pile driver's winch.

The aircraft had filled with mud and silt, and the upper wing was as heavy as concrete. Already rent in two, the airplane was dragged ashore piece by piece and piled on the bank, just out of the reach of high tide.

Merrill didn't wait for Cope's arrival to get to work. He enlisted help from the cannery workers to manhandle the 550-pound engine 100 yards to the little railway the company used to transport fish to the cannery. They transported the engine a mile and a half to the main cannery buildings and winched it upstairs to the cannery loft.

Merrill began dismantling the engine. This was the first air-cooled radial engine Merrill had ever worked on. The Whirlwind radial engine that propelled Charles Lindbergh's plane across the Atlantic that same year looked, to Lindbergh, "like a huge jewel" when he first saw it. Now Merrill could examine in detail another version of this first-ever truly reliable airplane engine, the motor his life depended upon.

He sawed a barrel in half, filled it with kerosene, and as he removed each part he submerged it in the kerosene to prevent rust. Merrill disassembled the Whirlwind engine and the airplane's instrument panel. The instruments were left to dry near a radiator in the cannery office.

The message that Merrill had sent to Cope asked him to hurry to the cannery to help clean and rebuild the engine. Cope left the day after he got the call for help. Merrill had asked Cope to bring a gallon of airplane dope, a couple of yards of fabric for patching, and a new propeller. But Cope hadn't become the operations manager of a bush flying outfit by being caught short in a crunch, so he decided to play it safe and bring along five times the repair materials Merrill requested. Cope brought five gallons of dope and fifteen yards of fabric. But even all this, Cope summed up later, "proved to be about one-tenth of what we needed."

Cope's five-day journey over sea and land to Lockanok with tools, materials, spare parts, and the two cannery executives Merrill had left behind was an expedition in itself. Nothing was flying out of Anchorage at that point. So from Anchorage the party took a Libby, McNeil & Libby boat down Cook Inlet to Iliamna Bay. At the twelve-mile portage between the bay and Iliamna Lake, which lies at the top of the Aleutian Peninsula, they loaded their baggage, aircraft materials, and tool bag onto two horses. The three men walked the portage, with Cope carrying the heavy laminated wood propeller.

The party crossed a 2,000-foot ridge in the Aleutian Range on a narrow mountain trail. The horse carrying the irreplaceable dope and tools was stumbling badly and Cope saw in his mind's eye the horse, dope, and tools careening down the slope. But they made it over the ridge, reached Iliamna village (Old Iliamna) at the eastern corner of the lake at 5 p.m. on June 24, and stayed there overnight. A small boat took them the length of the lake and down the Kvichak River to its mouth and then a few miles east to the cannery.

Cope was still optimistic. "Before we got to Lockanok I had learned from some fellows that we met on the river about what had happened to the plane, but I thought they surely didn't know what they were talking about. I was hoping hope against hope, I guess."

They arrived at Lockanok at midnight, "and I could see a pile of airplane laying out close to the dock where we landed. I saw the wings intact and still believed I was right in thinking the men had misinformed me. . . . Russ was glad to see me and started right away in telling me what had happened and what we would have to do. I told him I didn't think that it would be so bad, but Russ knew what he was talking about, and it surely was. . . . It turned out to be an awful job."

First came the engine. Cope had never seen anything quite like it. There was silt in every conceivable space, even in the hollow wrist pins that attached the connecting rods to the nine pistons. It took a week to recondition the motor; they spent a full day cleaning the crankshaft bearings alone, running them in gasoline and then oil, then gasoline again and again, to eliminate every trace of grit.

Likewise, all the instruments worked when Merrill and Cope were finished with them, except for the altimeter, the hairspring of which had rusted in half. They rebuilt the clock and made it work. Cope felt that "After this job was completed, Russel and I could have qualified for a mechanic's position in any place from a watch shop to a lumber yard."

The rest of the aircraft was piled on the beach, and there weren't enough of the right materials or tools to rebuild the airframe properly. The men decided to save their limited supplies of fabric for the fuselage, since it appeared to be the most heavily damaged part of the plane. That meant the wings had to be rebuilt with no new materials. And they had only one month to complete the work. After that, the cannery would close down and the loft they were using would be needed for storage.

"There we were," Cope said, "four wings to repair and nothing to repair them with. There were no more boats to come in that season from any port where we might get supplies. There were no more water-equipped airplanes in the territory to fly us supplies, and we could not waste the time taking a small boat from there to Anchorage for supplies, so we just had to repair the plane with what we had . . . a pocket knife, a hand saw, and a small plane we had borrowed from the cannery carpenters."

More problems awaited. The aircraft was dumped on the beach above the tide line, still upside down, on blocks. At least the wings were still in-

THE SECTION BEHIND THE PILOT'S COCKPIT, SIX FEET IN THE MIDDLE OF THE FUSELAGE, WAS ALMOST COMPLETELY GONE; A MASS OF PIANO WIRE AND STEEL TUBING WERE ALL THAT REMAINED.

tact. Merrill and Cope recruited four cannery workers to hold one half of the top wing while they extracted the last pins connecting that side of the wing to the struts. When the pins came away the weight of the wing overwhelmed the four men and Merrill and Cope, and it dropped on the men with a crash. There were holes in the wings and they were packed solid with silt from the river bottom. The wings were so heavy that six men were unable to hold one wing section up off the ground. They called upon more men to help remove the rest of the wing sections, manhandle them onto railway cars, and transport them to the cannery loft.

Merrill and Cope removed the fabric from the wings and cleaned out the sand. Intent on saving every scrap of fabric, they peeled the covering off the hard way: cutting it at the leading edge, reaching inside and cutting the lockstitch, and then stripping the fabric off. They laid the fabric out on the dock platform, washed it down with hoses, and scrubbed it with brooms. Then, handling it like raw silk, they hung it to best hold its shape while it dried.

Next came the four piles of broken ribs and spars. They saved every tack and straightened every nail they could. They also resorted to using shoe nails—five boxes of them—which, being wedge-shaped, tended to split the wood. So they drilled holes for the shoe nails, a precise and tedious routine.

Once the two cans of Lepage's glue donated by the cannery were used up, Merrill and Cope split open the glue cans and heated them on radiators to get every last drop. Their single instance of good fortune was the cannery's supply of seasoned straight-grained spruce, from which they made ribs and spliced the broken spars. Spruce was still the most common structural airframe material during the 1920s.

Throughout the wing rebuilding process, with their strict deadline approaching, Merrill and Cope were working from 7 a.m. to 10 p.m., with an hour off at noon. The grueling hours took their toll.

"Russ would eat as fast as he could and lay down for a little sleep," Cope wrote. "He would ask me to call him, but many times I would not do it. I would go back and work and let Russ sleep. He would wake up at about 2:00 or 2:30 and come dashing out to where I was, always apologizing for oversleeping and wondering why I did not wake him up. We kept this pace up until we had the wood work on the wings completed."

Restretching the old wing covering was like stretching an artist's canvas—after the painting had dried. Two small strips of wood laid on the edge of the fabric were grasped with pliers. It took several men pulling on the pliers to stretch the material enough to be close to covering the wing. They tacked the material in place, sewed fabric around the edges to make ends meet, patched holes, and finally lockstitched the wing.

Material for striping the wing—the tape reinforcements over each rib—was obtained by buying up all the sheets from Libby, McNeil & Libby and nearby canneries and making tape out of the linen. They used as little dope as possible—just enough to make the cloth stick.

They saved the worst for last. Assembling the complete fuselage had its tense moments: the tail appeared to have been stolen until it was found a quarter of a mile from the rest of the wreckage in some grass that had grown tall during the intervening weeks.

The section behind the pilot's cockpit, six feet in the middle of the fuselage, was almost completely gone; a mass of piano wire and steel tubing were all that remained. The Travel Air's steel tube fuselage was welded, not bolted. But the cannery had no welding equipment. Again, the canneries in the area donated items, and somehow the men pieced together a welding

Russel Merrill stands before the heavily damaged fuselage of *Anchorage No. 1* before he and Alonzo Cope repaired it at Lockanok in June and July of 1927. The fuselage was broken completely apart at the pilot's cockpit just to the right in this picture.

system. And again, the job of reusing mangled metal, like reusing old doped fabric, required meticulous teamwork.

Cope said: "We took this mass of wire and tubing apart. Each place the tubing was bent we cut in half with our hacksaw and laid out on the floor end-to-end. The whole thing was cut into about one hundred pieces. We straightened the pieces out and made a swage just the size the tubing should be. We would heat the tubing and drive the swage into it until the tubing was back to its original shape.

"After all the tubing was reshaped, I took some gas pipe, and on the lathe I turned out bushings to fit every joint that was to be made by the cutting and straightening we had done. We telescoped all these pieces together, drilled and pinned them, then welded every joint. Finally we got the tail surfaces of the fuselage connected with the cabin section."

A built-up structure as complicated as an aircraft frame is normally constructed on a jig, which ensures that the final dimensions and shape will be correct. Amazingly enough, the fuselage that Merrill and Cope painstakingly reassembled with nothing more than string, a plumb bob, and rulers for measuring turned out to be airworthy. The fifteen yards of airplane cloth Cope had brought with him covered the gap where the fuselage had been pulled apart. They had saved the airplane fabric for this purpose, knowing they wouldn't have enough dope left for it.

The only parts of the Travel Air that emerged from the river intact and undamaged were the pontoons, which were the only parts completely out of the water after the airplane flipped over.

Cope describes the final stages of the Travel Air's resurrection after the pontoon struts were straightened:

We put the landing gear under the fuselage, then carried the motor down and installed it. Then came the wings. They were carried down on the little railroad cars to where we were assembling, and our trouble almost began all over anew. A windstorm came up suddenly just as we were about to complete installing the wings and, had it not been for a number of the cannery crew, the ship would have blown away. Winds come up fast and furious on the Bering Sea, and they go as fast as they come.

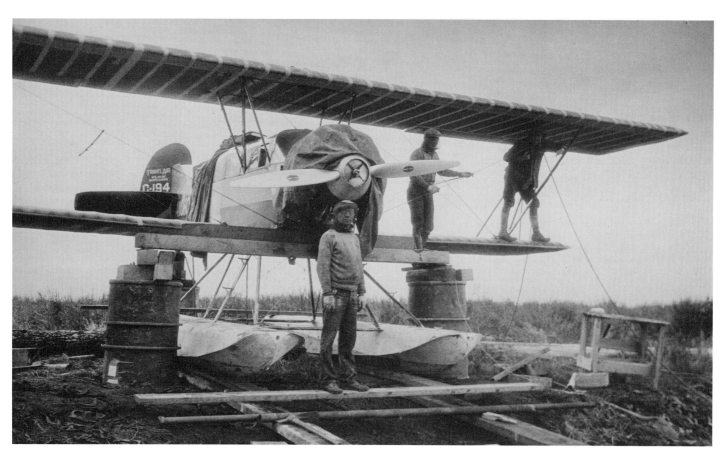

Workers rig the wings on *Anchorage No. 1* in late July 1927 after the airplane was rebuilt by Alonzo Cope and Russel Merrill at Lockanok cannery.

We worked until 12 o'clock that night getting the ship as ready as possible. We tied the plane down with several large ropes to the corner of the boathouse, and to four big pylons that lay on the ground beside it. We knew that if that ship blew away from where we had it anchored, the whole cannery would go and us with it; so it made no difference after that, and we lay down for a good rest. We were about to realize our dream of having this ship flying once again.

The next morning [July 28] we went back at 7 as usual to check our rigging and to run the motor. After everything was checked and all seemed to be OK, we started the motor. Thinking there might still be some sand in the motor, we did not hook the oil discharge line into the oil tank. We ran fifteen gallons of oil through the motor and onto the ground. That day we completely checked out the motor. Tomorrow was to be our test flight.

We got up the morning of the 29th at 3:30 to take advantage of the tide. We had placed the ship the night before on the beach just above high water mark and had placed skids before the ship so it would be easy to roll in the water. We reached the plane just a little bit before high water and had the ship in the water and all ready to go at 4 a.m.

But as we started to crank the motor, it failed us. We kept cranking and kept pushing the ship out, keeping it afloat, until the breakfast bell rang at 7:30. We had bid all the cannery crew goodbye the night before, thinking we would be away at 3:30 the next morning and would never again see the bunch of boys who helped us so faithfully through this job. But, lo and behold! We had to face them at breakfast again.

We hated to do this because about one-third of the men figured that the plane would never fly again. Then, when we had to go back again the next morning, the I-told-you-so came.

After we ate we laid down for an hour and took a little rest and went back to try our motor again. Evidently we had flooded out the motor at the very beginning, and in continual cranking it got stiff: all spark plugs had to come out; pour oil into the cylinders, then crank some more.

After breakfast we had new life; we knew that the motor was going to run. So Russ got into the cockpit and I got at the propeller, and we started all over anew. I pulled the motor through two or three times and Russ primed it just a little. I got at the crank and yelled "Contact."

The newly repaired Travel Air floats on the river at Lockanok. The man in the cockpit of *Anchorage No. 1* is Gordon MacKenzie, a pilot who happened to be working at the Lockanok cannery when the plane turned over. He helped in the rebuilding.

Russ threw on the switch, and in about three turns of the crank the motor went. You would have thought we were burning soft coal in the motor from the amount of smoke that came forth. The whole motor was drenched with cylinder oil: the cylinders were full, and so was the exhaust ring. But in a little while the smoke cleared up and the motor ran nicely.

Cope noted that by this time, the tide had moved back out and the airplane was standing in the mud, some five or six hundred yards from the water. While Merrill gunned the motor to propel the plane across the mud, Cope walked along and held onto the lower right wing, trying to help maneuver the plane across the mud and around several ditches. But the plane took off across the mud and was soon out of Cope's reach. The plane slid on the slick mud into one of the ditches—but powered up out of it and reached the water. From there, Merrill took off on the test flight of the airplane the men had just patched back together.

Cope continues his story:

Russ was gone some two hours. I was worried pink wondering what had happened. I thought of a million things that could have happened. There we would be stranded. And, too, I was worried about losing the ship after all our efforts. For all I knew, probably Russ was dead. I knew that he must have landed somewhere or he would have been back. Probably the fuselage buckled on landing. Probably a strut gave way. In fact, I didn't know what to think when he did not return.

Finally he returned in two hours with a big smile, saying the ship flew as well as ever and was rigged perfectly, with the exception of the right wing being just a little heavy.

We had lunch and then said goodbye to all the cannery crew again; the cook and everyone else, and the cannery superintendent Mr. Smith, Mrs. Smith and the twins. We refueled, packed all of our stuff into the ship, and took off for Anchorage. It was July 29—41 days since the plane was wrecked.

We were out about thirty minutes and noticed in our path a storm brewing over Iliamna Lake. There was no getting out of this storm other than going back to Lockanok and we did not want to do that—once away from that place we wanted to stay away. If we went back to Lockanok we stood a chance of having our ship blown away a second time. So we headed into the storm.

There the ship was tested! We were both scared stiff, for we thought surely the wings would come off, the way the ship pitched and rolled. We would look out and see the undoped fabric on the fuselage fluttering against the piano wires, and glance out at the wing tips and see them vibrate as the ship would toss, wondering if our one coat of dope would hold. The air was too rough to fly down close to the water, so we had to climb above the clouds to an altitude of 10,000 feet.

There we were, above the storm with a ship questionable throughout, from the motor to the tail skid, including instruments. We flew above the storm two hours when finally we checked our position against Mount Iliamna. . . . We decided to try to find Iliamna village [Old Iliamna].

We came down through the clouds little by little, from hole to hole, always keeping openings enough in the clouds visible to climb back up if it was as rough near the ground there as it was where we climbed up. As we came down we found the air smoother. We flew near the shoreline and finally came to Iliamna village and landed.

We were tickled to death to be nearer Anchorage than we had been in some month and a half. We anchored the ship in a small lagoon where we knew it would be safe from any wind that might come up and turned in at the Post Office (that being the roadhouse) for our night's rest.

We didn't sleep much that night, for the storm that we were over that day reached Iliamna village that night and never in my life have I heard the wind blow so hard. We listened to the wind blow and wondered what we should do. The ship was anchored a mile or so from where we were sleeping, and, were we at the ship, we could do nothing. So we decided to wait until morning to go near it.

The next morning I ran down toward the river, took a boat, and rowed to where I could see the ship. And there she stood anchored in the little lagoon. . . . I rushed back to our "hotel" and reported this to Russ. We had a nice breakfast, Russ shaved, and we went down to the ship to get away.

Anchorage No. 1 sits off of Iliamna village on July 30, 1927. Russel Merrill and Alonzo Cope were forced by a storm to land there overnight on their trip back to Anchorage after rebuilding the plane at Lockanok.

Merrill and Cope first towed *Anchorage No. 1* by motorboat out onto Iliamna Lake to get plenty of room for takeoff. The wind did its best to capsize the plane as it was towed. At one point, Merrill leaped from the cockpit and out onto the right wing tip, forcing the wing back down before the wind could finish lifting it up and over.

Cope tells about their further adventures after getting out onto the lake:

We debated whether to take off or return to the village. By that time it was 1 p.m.

A thick lot of clouds were overhead and a stiff wind was blowing. The lake had gotten very rough and we were in the only smooth spot on the whole lake, a little cove in the shelter of two mountains.

We had wired Anchorage on the 29th that we were leaving Lockanok and should reach Anchorage about 6 o'clock that evening. This being the 30th, and almost 24 hours overdue then, we knew that Mrs. Merrill and everybody in Anchorage would be worried. Iliamna village had no radio, so we could not report our whereabouts.

So we decided to take a chance. . . . Mr. Faust, the postmaster at Iliamna who owned the little motorboat we had used in the towing, was helping us. He let his boat serve as an anchor. We could not crank our motor there because when we cranked the ship it would creep up on his boat; we would not dare crank the ship and try to taxi for the simple reason that we could only taxi in one direction [into the wind], and that would be straight toward shore.

The wind was then blowing so hard we were afraid to even turn our ship broadside to it. So we let our ship drift back some 1,500 feet from the shore. The shore was a bluff about 500 feet high, behind which was a small bench about one mile wide; then the mountains towered up some 2,500 to 3,000 feet high.

We gave Mr. Faust the signal, and he cut us loose. I cranked the ship, standing on the right pontoon just behind the propeller and ahead of the lower wing. The motor idled along some three or four minutes. Russ increased the revolutions to about 1,000 rpm to warm the motor up more rapidly, and in doing this the ship started creeping toward shore.

Russ knew the ship would soon be too close to shore to take off so he opened the throttle wide. I had thought he was going to taxi up close to shore, cut the gun, and let the ship drift out again. But when he gave it the gun it came up on the step and was off the water in about two seconds.

There I stood, out on the pontoon, just ahead of the right lower wing. I pushed the crank into the cabin through the open window, and started climbing down the pontoon struts to enter the cabin from the left side, where the only door to the cabin was. We cranked the motor from the right side, thus making it necessary to either climb over the top of the cabin and down onto the left wing and into the cabin, or under the ship.

I immediately decided to go under the ship, thinking I might obstruct Russ's view by climbing over the top. On climbing under the fuselage my head had to go past the exhaust pipe and the motor, which did not suit me by any means. The purr was not steady. The motor was cold and Russ was climbing the ship as steep as it could climb.

While I was on the struts I looked down to see what we were going over, hoping I would see water, so that if the motor did quit, we would be able to land. But what I saw was a bluff, and then the trees began. We were over the bluff and up on the bench, and Russ was making a right turn to get more altitude before crossing the mountains.

THE WIND DID ITS BEST TO CAPSIZE THE PLANE AS IT WAS TOWED ONTO THE LAKE. AT ONE POINT, MERRILL LEAPED FROM THE COCKPIT AND OUT ONTO THE RIGHT WING TIP, FORCING THE WING BACK DOWN BEFORE THE WIND COULD FINISH LIFTING IT UP AND OVER.

The scenery was pretty, the motor was working better, and I was better satisfied, knowing we were once again in the air and headed for Anchorage, I didn't care if I was on the tail skid, the pontoon struts, the upper wing, or in the cabin.

I climbed up on the left wing and I could see a worried look on Russ's face. He was looking out over the right side of the fuselage. When he looked to the left and saw me on the left wing, I don't think I ever saw a man quite so happy. A big broad smile spread over his face and he yelled.

I climbed in the cabin, Russ settled down to his controls, we climbed to 11,000 feet over the clouds and headed for Anchorage. We flew above the clouds for an hour and a half, took our bearings from the Alaska Range, and knew we would come out at Anchorage after a while.

In about thirty minutes the clouds began to thin out. Next was sunshine. We circled Anchorage one time and watched the cars start for Lake Spenard, where we were to land, some four miles away. I think everybody in town had their automobile warmed up, ready to start for Lake Spenard. The road was jammed for a mile we could see.

We landed at Lake Spenard at 5:30 p.m. July 30 . . . just a month and eleven days, lacking thirty minutes, from the time Russ had left Spenard for Bristol Bay.

Mrs. Merrill was at Lake Spenard, and had been there some time. She was much worried about the non-appearance of the plane. We anchored the plane safely there and went to Anchorage to try to forget our plane for a few days at least.

ANCHORAGE AIR TRANSPORT, Inc.

ANCHORAGE, ALASKA

Passenger and Express RATES

ANCHORAGE TO AND FROM	PASSENGERS EACH			EXPRESS PER LB.
	ONE	TWO	THREE	
AKIAK	$500.00	$400.00	$300.00	$1.00
BETHEL	500.00	400.00	300.00	1.00
NOME	750.00	500.00	350.00	1.00
McGRATH	250.00	200.00	185.00	.50
OPHIR	265.00	212.50	190.00	.50
TAKOTNA	265.00	212.50	190.00	
IDITAROD	300.00	250.00	225.00	
FLAT	300.00	250.00	225.00	
ILIAMNA	300.00	250.00	225.00	
SELDOVIA	250.00	200.00	185.00	
NINILCHICK	125.00	100.00	95.00	
KASILOF	100.00	85.00	75.00	.25
TUSTAMENA	125.00	100.00	95.00	.25
KENAI	80.00	70.00	60.00	.25
SEWARD	80.00	70.00	60.00	.25
WILLOW CREEK	50.00	40.00	35.00	.15
MOOSE CREEK	50.00	40.00	35.00	.15
WASILLA	35.00	30.00	25.00	.15
SUSITNA	40.00	30.00	25.00	.15
TYONIC	45.00	35.00	30.00	.15
TRADING BAY	50.00	40.00	35.00	.15
LAKE CHACKCHAMANA	125.00	100.00	95.00	.25
SLEITMUTE	250.00	200.00	185.00	.50

Baggage allowance 20 lbs. each passenger.

Furs and Gold Dust double Express rate.

A. A. SHONBECK, Manager

ANCHORAGE WAS A DIFFICULT BASE TO FLY FROM. IT WAS SURROUNDED BY A VAST UNMADE BED OF TOWERING MOUNTAINS, PARTICULARLY TO THE WEST. A FLIGHT FROM ANCHORAGE TO ANY OUTLYING DISTRICT SUCH AS THE KUSKOKWIM, THE CANNERIES OF BRISTOL BAY, OR THE SEWARD PENINSULA MEANT CROSSING OR CIRCUMNAVIGATING THESE MOUNTAIN BARRIERS. LITTLE OF THIS FORBIDDING LANDSCAPE HAD BEEN MAPPED BY 1927.

Anchorage Air Transport's rates reflected the harshness of the territory. The Anchorage-Nome fare was $750 for a single passenger or $350 for each member of a party of three. Meanwhile, routine commutes to nearby places like Susitna could cost as little as $25 for each of three passengers. Freight to Akiak, Bethel, or Nome cost a dollar a pound; double for furs or gold dust.

It was because of the rugged landscape and changeable weather that Merrill had found himself rebuilding the company's two Travel Air planes more than he flew them from March until August of 1927. Now Merrill and Cope checked over *Anchorage No. 1's* Lockanok repairs at their home base. The cabin plane was thoroughly examined and repaired. Dope was applied over the bare fabric behind the cockpit, although the capital letters spelling Anchorage remained incomplete. Merrill flight-tested the plane successfully on August 5.

Anchorage No. 2, the smaller plane, was still not back from the Candle area, where it had crash-landed April 5. But with Merrill now the company's only pilot, this plane was not unduly missed. In early June, AAT's other pilot, Ed Young, had done something about one of the most difficult problems facing Alaska fliers. He left AAT to join the state Road Commission, where he would recommend future airfield sites. The company hated to

Overleaf: A rate sheet gives air travel prices for passengers and freight (express) in the Anchorage region in 1927. Anchorage Air Transport was the only air service covering that area in the 1920s.

lose Young, but now there was a better chance of getting good airfields.

The motor from damaged *Anchorage No. 2* arrived a few days after *Anchorage No. 1* was fully operational again. The Whirlwind motor that had been taken by dogsled from Candle to Unalakleet had then been sent back to Anchorage via St. Michael and the Yukon River. Repairing it became Alonzo Cope's late-summer project.

Starting August 6, Merrill barnstormed around Anchorage and then undertook survey flights to areas that had important implications for the future of aviation out of Anchorage.

One series of flights started as an August 10 excursion on behalf of Gus Gelles's Alaska Glacier Tours Association to Tustumena Lake on the Kenai Peninsula, where the association had a big-game hunting camp. Merrill found a site for a landing strip that would enable aircraft to ferry larger loads in and out on wheels than could be supported on floats. The next day Merrill flew in work crews to clear the site he had scouted on Tustumena Lake and a site he had identified on Eklutna Lake.

Two Army Air Service officers arrived in Anchorage at the end of August to look for military airfield sites. Lieutenant Jack O'Connell and a Lieutenant Davidson scouted the city from the air with Merrill, then looked over AAT's equipment and facilities and filed a report outlining their favorable impressions. But it was not until World War II that the Army Air Corps built the airfield that eventually became Elmendorf Air Force Base at Anchorage, the key refueling stop for trans-Arctic flights to Russia.

Merrill's familiarity with Anchorage's winding seacoast paid off later that year when returning from McGrath with three passengers. He found Anchorage fogged in under a fifty-foot ceiling. He followed the water for some distance, then turned back and flew low over the shoreline, gauging

THE *ANCHORAGE TIMES*, ALERTED BY AN IMPRESSED PASSENGER, DESCRIBED MERRILL'S MANEUVER IN FINDING THE AIRFIELD THROUGH LOW-LYING FOG AS FLYING "WITH THE ACCURACY OF A SHARPSHOOTER" OVER THE MASS OF TELEPHONE WIRES THAT BORDERED THE AIRSTRIP.

his exact position directly opposite the Anchorage airstrip. At that point he banked sharply to the right, pulled up over the tops of a line of trees and telephone lines that had been invisible moments before in the fog, and flared down onto the field. The *Anchorage Times,* alerted by an impressed passenger, described the maneuver as flying "with the accuracy of a sharpshooter" over the mass of telephone wires that bordered the airstrip.

There was plenty of business in the Kuskokwim. Time was money in this immense territory. Trappers bringing their furs in to Bethel and Akiak from trap lines all along the Kuskokwim River, or returning to the trap lines, were anxious to take advantage of the speed of air travel. For miners, the fastest possible transportation could be critical to staking and working claims. During the long winter, towns like Bethel were cut off from the outside world.

At this stage in the development of Alaska aviation, the way to the Kuskokwim from Anchorage was northwest through Rainy Pass and then on to McGrath along the route to Ruby and Nome. This meant flying well north of the ideal straight line from Anchorage. The Mount Spurr region of the Alaska Range blocked direct access west from Anchorage to the Kuskokwim.

Maps published before 1930 did not show the locations of the mountains and glaciers within that 10,000-square-mile area. Ever since his first westward flight, Merrill had harbored the hope of exploring this matrix of sawtooth mountain peaks. He knew that if he could penetrate this barrier and fly straight to the Kuskokwim, he could save seventy-five miles each way.

Merrill finally made that flight November 6, 1927. The weather was good, and he flew a straight compass course over the mountains from Anchorage toward Akiak. Passing over Cook Inlet and the tundra east of Mount Spurr, he climbed to gain enough altitude to clear the mountains. Merrill passed over the first set of broken ridges and entered the maze of rocky slopes and serpentine valleys.

For miles, nearing the end of reliable detail on his maps, he flew closer to the edge of the known Alaska Range. Far below appeared an elongated body of water, large for a glacial lake. This was Chakachamna Lake, the eastern end of which had been surveyed only the previous summer by the U.S. Geological Survey party led by Steven R. Capps.

Then Merrill passed into the unknown. As he crossed the mountains, he sighted a winding course to the south which he thought could be the pass he was hoping for. He could not investigate further then but continued on to Akiak, where he had business.

The next day he flew between Akiak and Bethel. On November 8, he set off across the range again, headed back to Anchorage, carrying three passengers. This time he flew low. As he approached the mountains he passed over two unmapped lakes that he logged as Two Lake and Upper Two Lake. Then he entered the granite core of the range through a valley that looked promising. Confronted with converging walls of rock and ice, he was forced to climb higher, exploring canyon after canyon. Each was a blind alley.

Finally he found a canyon that penetrated the crest of the divide, but it, too, appeared to be blocked by a wall of granite. Although no clear passageway was visible, Merrill thought he might be able to get through.

Just as he approached the end of the canyon and thought he was blocked from proceeding farther, he saw an opening to the south. Hidden by a bend in the canyon, it revealed itself as Merrill flew toward it. He banked and

IN THE THIN MINUS-30 DEGREE AIR, MERRILL KEPT THE AIRCRAFT STEADY FROM HIS OPEN COCKPIT AS HE FOCUSED THE BIG, HEAVY CAMERA WITH THICK, FUR-LINED MITTENS. DESPITE THE SEVERE CONDITIONS, HE RETURNED WITH A SERIES OF PHOTOGRAPHS OF MOUNT SPURR AND OF THE PASS HE HAD DISCOVERED.

Merrill Pass in the Alaska Range west of Anchorage provides a direct low-elevation route through the mountains to the Kuskokwim region. The pass is entered by turning left at the valley in the center-left of the picture. The diagonal lines are caused by the wing rigging on the plane flown by Russel Merrill when he took this photo November 10, 1927, just two days after he discovered the new route.

turned sharply to the right and came through safely to the other side of the Alaska Range. The valley floors dropped away. Beyond lay Chakachamna Lake and the river that found its source there.

Two days later, Merrill made a second flight through the pass, this time flying alone. Then he continued east by northeast along Chakachamna Lake and directly over Mount Spurr, becoming the first pilot to fly over the 11,000-foot volcano. His Travel Air took him over the top at an altitude of 13,000 feet.

Merrill carried his camera with him to take pictures of this largely unknown area. In the thin minus-30-degree air, he kept the aircraft steady from his open cockpit as he focused the big, heavy camera with thick, fur-lined mittens. Despite the severe conditions, Merrill returned with a series of photographs of the mountain, the pass he had discovered, and other features of the Mount Spurr region.

With discovery of this shorter route across the Alaska Range, flights to and from the Kuskokwim could be made in a day, whereas flying around through Rainy Pass often took two days. The cost of a one-way flight be-

This is a view through Merrill Pass, which offers a low-level flying route when clouds cover the tops of the nearby mountains, which range from 6,500 to 12,000 feet elevation. The floor of the pass is at 3,000 feet.

This is the view while leaving Merrill Pass, headed west. The photo was taken by Russel Merrill on November 10, 1927, from the open cockpit of *Anchorage No. 1*.

tween Anchorage and Bethel or Akiak dropped by one hundred dollars, which increased travel through the Alaska Range. This low-elevation pass—only 3,000 feet—was a boon to aircraft of the time, which lacked accurate altimeters, let alone instrument flying capability. Merrill Pass became an official landmark with publication of the 1930 government maps.

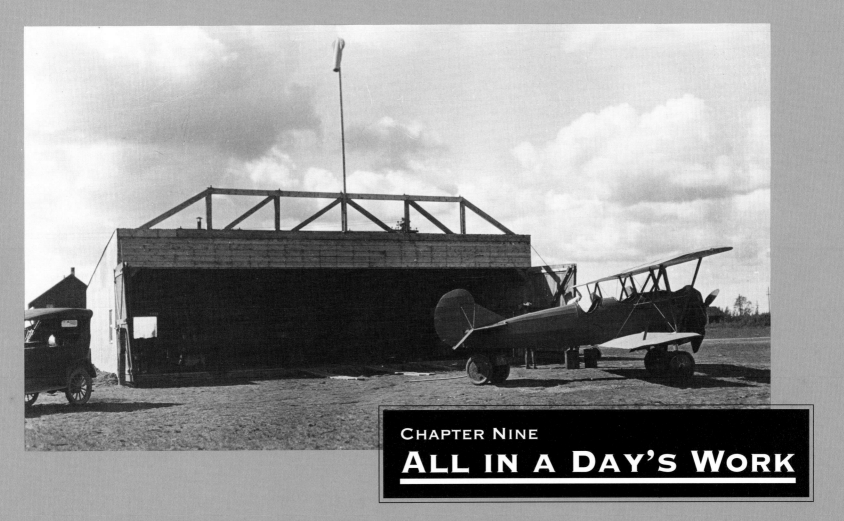

CHAPTER NINE

ALL IN A DAY'S WORK

MERRILL TESTED THE REBUILT *ANCHORAGE NO. 2*

ON THE DAY AFTER CHRISTMAS 1927 AND

FOUND IT AIRWORTHY. THE TWO-PLANE FLEET

WAS ONCE AGAIN COMPLETE.

THE DISTRESS SIGNAL WAS SO FAINT THE SENDER COULDN'T BE SURE IT WOULD BE RECEIVED. WALTER KOTOFF, A YOUNG RUSSIAN, HAD MUSHED THIRTY MILES UP COOK INLET IN THE DEAD OF WINTER FROM NINILCHIK TO USE THE HAM RADIO ON THE WILLIAMSON FOX FARM, ONLY TO FIND THE PRIMITIVE SPARK-COIL UNIT WASN'T WORKING. HE PATCHED IT UP AND SENT HIS MESSAGE: MISS BESS HOWE, THE SCHOOLTEACHER AT NINILCHIK, HAD SHOT HERSELF IN THE STOMACH WHILE CLEANING HER REVOLVER THE DAY BEFORE, NOVEMBER 20, 1927.

With no receiver—only a transmitter—Kotoff had no way of knowing if his call for help had been received. Assuming it hadn't, he returned to Ninilchik over the winter trail in minus-20-degree temperatures, arriving exhausted.

Kotoff found Miss Howe alone and deteriorating fast. Her advancing delirium told Kotoff she was on the verge of being overcome by blood poisoning. He then borrowed a small gas boat and pounded sixty miles in rough water down the inlet to Seldovia to get help. There he learned his wireless message had been received after all and that a plane had been dispatched to rescue the teacher. Kotoff collapsed from exhaustion and relief.

Ninilchik is on the west coast of the Kenai Peninsula, 115 miles southwest of Anchorage. Merrill was far away in Fairbanks with the cabin plane when he got word of the urgent wireless. Fairbanks was socked in for the day, but Merrill was in Anchorage the following day and left for Ninilchik the next morning with two passengers and Dr. Arthur Haverstock of the Anchorage government hospital.

After dropping his passengers at way points, Merrill landed on a lake that he thought was a couple of miles from Ninilchik. "As a matter of fact,"

Overleaf: The first airplane hangar at Anchorage was a wood frame structure with galvanized iron sides and roof. Anchorage Air Transport completed the building—measuring forty feet by fifty feet, with an eleven-foot ceiling—at the airfield in November 1927.

he reported later, "the distance proved to be six miles, much to our sorrow, since we had to walk."

Dr. Haverstock found nine internal wounds caused by the single shot through Bess Howe's abdomen; the bullet had exited through her back. She was in a highly critical condition from blood poisoning. After initial treatment at her cabin, the doctor made her as comfortable as possible for the night.

The next morning he injected her with morphine to ease her pain for the trip to the plane and on to Anchorage. The landscape from Ninilchik to the lake is hilly, and there was no trail. Merrill and the doctor put her on a dogsled and found enough men to lift her and the sled over windfalls and bumps. Dr. Haverstock had to rest several times before they managed to climb the hills on the way back to the lake.

Merrill tells how they readied the plane for the Thanksgiving Day mercy flight back to Anchorage:

The emergency cook stove we carry in the plane was too small to warm the motor in less than two or three hours, so we brought a Yukon wood stove from town. The wood we cut for the stove had so much moisture in it that all the wiring of the motor was damp by the time the motor was warm, hence it was very hard to start.

After finally starting the motor, I taxied the ship out on the lake and happened to run through some overflow water that was completely covered with snow. This put a six-inch coating of slush ice on the bottom of the skis. We had to lift one side of the plane at a time and scrape this off with my hunting knife. The ship weighs about 3,000 pounds loaded, and there were only three of us, including the musher, to do the lifting. However, it wasn't quite as bad as it sounds, as we lifted on the wingtip, so we had a lot of leverage.

One of the two magnetos failed to function at all because of the bath of wet, warm air it received during the warming of the motor. But here was the sick girl, six miles from town and in desperate need of surgical attention. So the doctor loaded the girl in and I opened the throttle, trusting that the magneto would get us home. It was sundown (3 p.m.) when we finally took off.

The flight, as described by Dr. Haverstock, was "rough!"

"I have never experienced a trip like it. It was to be expected that my patient would be ill, but I was very sick, too. We would be sailing along nicely when all of a sudden we would drop a hundred feet or more in an instant. The delay at the lake caused us to start at dusk, and it grew very dark on the way home, making us apprehensive of our location."

Arriving over Anchorage, Merrill circled several times to alert the townspeople and hospital staff. Cars converged on the airstrip to illuminate it with their headlights. After checking the smokestack at the railroad power plant for wind direction, Merrill landed, and an ambulance took Bess Howe to the government hospital. Her life was saved.

In November 1927, Anchorage Air Transport completed framing and roofing of the city's first airplane hangar, a forty-foot by fifty-foot building with an eleven-foot ceiling. The building immediately housed a project that would have been nearly impossible to carry out at that time of year without the hangar: rebuilding of the wrecked *Anchorage No. 2.* The building contractor was still installing the hangar's doors while the smaller Travel Air craft that had been wrecked back in April near Candle continued to materialize in bits and pieces.

The damaged motor from *Anchorage No. 2* had arrived in Anchorage during August, before the hangar went up. Alonzo Cope had overhauled it and set it aside. The fuselage, shipped from Kiwalik (near Candle) by boat to Seward and up to Anchorage by train, arrived in November and was restored with the expert assistance of Charlie Bisel. Finally, new wings, motor mounts, and landing gear, plus wing struts and all the necessary fittings, arrived from the Travel Air factory at Wichita in time for the job to be completed before Christmas.

For the first time, an Anchorage Air Transport ship had been overhauled in a facility built for that purpose, rather than in the open on some far, windy shore with only the most basic of tools. An airline flies on the skills of its mechanics, and AAT finally had a workshop worthy of the talents of mechanic Alonzo Cope.

Merrill tested the rebuilt *Anchorage No. 2* on the day after Christmas 1927 and found it airworthy. The two-plane fleet was once again complete, though Merrill still was the company's sole pilot since Ed Young had taken the job with the state Road Commission in June.

On March 1, 1928, Matt A. Nieminen joined AAT, again giving the company a second pilot. Nieminen was a seasoned commercial pilot from Minnesota, holder of commercial flying license 2232. Though he had no cold-weather experience (he had been flying in Mexico for several years), a single check flight with Merrill in *Anchorage No. 2* on March 7 confirmed Nieminen's competence.

His first trip for AAT the next day proved his worth to the company. It was a fur-transporting job, a type of assignment Merrill had carried out before.

THE BULKY FURS WERE PACKED IN BALES. MANY OF THEM HAD TO BE CARRIED OUTSIDE THE PLANES, TIED TO STRUTS AND TO THE FUSELAGES.

Sacks of furs are lashed to the fuselage of *Anchorage No. 2*. Russel Merrill flew this load of furs through fog and snow from Bethel to Anchorage on January 27, 1928, making three stops on the way.

Nieminen, flying No. 2, accompanied Merrill, who was flying the cabin plane, to Bethel. Merrill and Nieminen flew back with more than half a ton of furs, worth $100,000.

The bulky furs were packed in bales. Many of them had to be carried outside the planes, tied to struts and to the fuselages. The drag caused by the furs reduced their airspeed, and they arrived in Anchorage too late to connect with the train heading to Seward to meet the southbound boat. So they flew on to Lawing, an intermediate rail stop, and intercepted the train.

The furs made the southbound boat, traveling in time to reach the all-important fur auction March 21 in Seattle. The shipment was insured from Bethel to Seattle by the Seattle Fur Exchange, and Merrill understood it was the first insured air freight shipment in Alaska.

One of the responsibilities of a bush pilot is to serve as a lifeline to

Russel Merrill, fur mukluks on his feet, prepares to climb into the open cockpit of the Travel Air cabin plane on March 10, 1928. He was on his way from Anchorage to Lawing with a load of furs to intercept the train that would take the furs to Seward for shipment to auction in Seattle.

MERRILL WAS FLYING FURS OUT OF BETHEL WHEN HE SAW A SIGN IN THE SNOW ALONGSIDE A CLEARING. IT WAS ASSEMBLED FROM BURLAP SACKING, WITH A SERIES OF SMALL STICKS ARRANGED ON IT. AS HE FLEW LOW HE MADE OUT THE WORDS NEED VACCINE.

trappers and hunters in the wild. Once the pilot has agreed to appear at a certain place on a certain day with supplies and gear, his promptness could mean the difference between life and death.

This burden was especially acute in the case of George Shaben, a deaf trapper. He was one of the first trappers to be flown in to Chakachamna Lake. After Merrill flew him to the lake in mid-January 1928, Shaben, an accomplished woodsman, built a cabin on its shores and lived there through the winter. Merrill frequently flew over the area on his way to or from the alpine gateway of Merrill Pass and checked on him. Shaben stayed in the region for years, supplied from the air and moved by plane to different trapping sites.

In January Merrill made two flights into the Bethel area, and the next month he received the following lively letter from the village of Quithlook (or Kwethluk, as it is spelled today). The village is situated eight miles northeast of Bethel, where the Kwethluk River flows into the Kuskokwim.

My dear Mr. Merrill:

This is to ask you if it would be at all possible for you to come a little closer to our village the next time you fly past. Some of the door jambs on the schoolhouse are permanently damaged by the avalanche of your native humanity that hit them when they heard your plane. If you could come a bit closer I don't know whether their joy would stay in bounds or not—or the school be left standing.

Why not come for a visit? My river is smoother ice than the Kuskokwim, and just as strong! Couldn't your engine jar loose a screw or something— not a big one, only a tiny little one that just had to be tightened at Quithlook village? I can't promise you a brass band to welcome you, but I might per-

suade Paul to play "Glory Glory Hallelujah" on his accordion. The Kochpuks
would be sure to play "Why Did I Kiss That Girl" on their new orthophonic.
They've about worn the record through already, but for such a grand occa-
sion they might play it once more!

Why don't you come a week later? I'm giving my long-talked-of dance
on March 10, and everyone is invited provided they bring their own bedroll
and dog feed. Go on back and bring in another load next week.

My chief, Harry Jackson, is the bearer of this. Not only is he the most
influential native on this river, but the best scout. He'll tell you all you
want to know about landing places in Quithlook!

Sincerely,

Ellie May Deter

On April 6, having missed Ellie May's much-anticipated dance at
Quithlook School, Merrill was flying more furs out of Bethel when he saw a
sign in the snow alongside a clearing. It was assembled from burlap sacking,
with a series of small sticks arranged on it.

As he flew low he made out the words NEED VACCINE. He landed the
plane in the clearing and learned that Miss Deter's school was asking for the
medicine. After finding out what was needed, he flew on to Bethel and arranged to get the serum to the school.

The U.S. Geological Survey, its interest in the Mount Spurr region whet-
ted by Merrill's aerial photographs and descriptions of a pass through the
Alaska Range, hired Anchorage Air Transport in 1928 to fly some supplies
and personnel to the head of Chakachamna Lake. The airlift would be a first
for the Survey. The rest of the Survey's crew and equipment would be brought

in by pack train.

The agency had surveyed the region in 1927, looking for a pass across the range. Hearing of Merrill's discovery, topographic engineer R. H. Sargent wrote Merrill: "This, of course, is the coveted goal for which we were striving but unfortunately we were unable to reach because of the difficulties of travel, which consumed so much of our time that it was impossible to proceed further."

On Saturday June 9, Matt Nieminen flew the first of three members of the Survey, plus a first shipment of air freight that eventually added up to 2,600 pounds, to the lake in the open plane, *Anchorage No. 2*. Four additional flights finished the airlift by Sunday afternoon.

The pack train left Saturday as well, crossing Cook Inlet by launch to Trading Bay, just east of Mount Spurr, and then taking a trail cut the previous summer to the lake head. The four men and fourteen horses faced difficult conditions on the trail. Deep snow covered the land above timberline, and any pastureland that might have provided food for the horses was buried. The pack train arrived at the camp in three weeks. Those who had flown were there in ninety minutes.

Chapter Ten

Stranded in the Arctic: 1928

Have enough rice cooked with me to last four days anyway. Hope to make Barrow or a native home, but rather doubt whether I can. Dearest love to my wife, boys and two fine brothers.

— From Russel Merrill's logbook; written just before he set off on his survival trek toward Barrow, May 24, 1928

HOLLYWOOD CAME CALLING IN THE SPRING OF 1928, BRINGING THE GLAMOUR AND EXCITEMENT OF THE MOVIES AND A BIG BOOST TO THE NORTHERN ECONOMY. THE FOX FILM EXPEDITION WAS IN ALASKA TO RECORD SCENES OF ESKIMO LIFE, GO WHALING WITH THE NATIVES ON THE ARCTIC OCEAN, AND FILM NATURE'S ANNUAL NORTHLAND MELODRAMA, THE SPRING BREAKUP OF ICE ABOVE THE ARCTIC CIRCLE.

Wien Alaska Airways of Fairbanks offered Anchorage Air Transport half the work of ferrying the Fox crew from Fairbanks to Barrow, the northernmost settlement in the United States. The proposition sounded heaven-sent, the timing just right for AAT. The airline was now fully equipped and debt free, having paid off $4,000 worth of new equipment. It had done $8,000 worth of business in April against only $2,000 of overhead.

On the Barrow trips, Merrill would fly *Anchorage No. 1*, the cabin plane, staying within sight of the most cautious, safety-conscious pilot, Noel Wien. Wien would fly his Stinson *Detroiter,* another modern enclosed cabin ship, which Wien had bought from arctic explorer Hubert Wilkins.

Both planes would be on wheels because the field at Fairbanks was free of snow and they anticipated a clear landing area on the ice at Barrow as well. Flying over the white desert of arctic Alaska with wheels, which are worse than useless in the snow, would be risky. Noel Wien's Stinson was at least shod with oversized tires for better buoyancy on soft surfaces. But to Anchorage Air Transport, the excursion seemed less dangerous than the trips the company made practically every day through the mountain ranges surrounding Anchorage.

Merrill met Virgil Hart, the Fox Film manager, in Anchorage, and took

Overleaf: A Fox Film crew was in Alaska in spring 1928 to film Eskimo life, whaling, and the ice breakup in the Arctic. Ready to be flown by Russel Merrill (right) from Fairbanks to Barrow are Fox Film manager Virgil Hart (center) and Alaska guide Jack Robertson.

The Fox Film Expedition stands ready to depart Weeks Field in Fairbanks on May 13, 1928, for Barrow. Wien Alaska Airways had the contract and gave Anchorage Air Transport half the work. At left is AAT's Travel Air Model CW (*Anchorage No. 1*); at right is Noel Wien's Stinson SB-1 *Detroiter*.

Hart and Captain Jack Robertson, the party's experienced Alaska guide, up for two local flights on May 7. Five days later, he flew the two to Fairbanks while the other members of the party and the camera equipment traveled north by railway.

On May 13, the two planes were ready to fly to Barrow. Hart and Robertson flew with Merrill; cameraman Charles G. Clarke and his equipment went with Wien. Each ship carried about 800 pounds. With that load, neither plane could surmount the Endicott Mountains, so they would have to thread their way through the passes. Leaving Fairbanks in clear weather, they flew together at 6,000 feet, crossing the Yukon River and covering the 195 miles to the village of Wiseman without incident. They landed on a

As Russel Merrill warms up Anchorage No.1 to leave Fairbanks for Barrow, members of the Fox Film Expedition pose before the plane. From left are Fox Film manager Virgil Hart, film director Ewing Scott, cameraman Charles Clarke, and guide Jack Robertson. Hart and Robertson flew with Merrill.

gravel bar, refueled, and had dinner.

The weather at Wiseman was good. But with no radio at Barrow, there was no way of knowing the conditions to the north. The planes took off after two hours at Wiseman and crossed the Endicott Mountains in an air temperature of 15 degrees. Once past the mountains, the two ships were soon over flat, barren tundra.

About 5 p.m.—some four hours out of Wiseman—they hit low clouds and fog. Within minutes the land was obscured. With no visible break in the murk ahead, the pilots didn't dare go on. But they were past the point of no

Russel Merrill's *Anchorage No. 1* sits on the river bed at Wiseman on May 13,
1928, after a flight from Fairbanks. The weather was clear when this plane
and Noel Wien's Stinson left later in the day for Barrow, but changed for the
worse after they crossed the mountains.

Noel Wien's Stinson and *Anchorage No. 1* (at left) were forced to land May 13, 1928, on a frozen lake on the arctic plain south of Barrow because of heavy fog and low fuel. The Stinson's large-size tires permitted it to take off the next day, but the standard-size tires of *Anchorage No. 1* sank in the snow.

return, with insufficient fuel to go back to Wiseman. They had to land. Arriving over a series of frozen lakes, Noel Wien made two attempts to land on one of them before he touched down in deep, soft snow. Both pilots knew they might not be able to take off again, but with the fog closing in, there was no choice. Merrill circled and landed nearby.

That night, some of the men slept in the airplanes' cabins and the others slept in sleeping bags on the snow. When they awoke, they found that the fog had lifted and a crust had formed on the snow.

Wien's *Detroiter*, with the larger tires, had the best chance of getting airborne. He decided to try for Barrow to get help and shovels to dig a runway for Merrill's Travel Air. The heavy camera equipment was removed from Wien's plane and only Virgil Hart went with him. A head wind and the crust on the snow helped Wien take off. He circled, looking for landmarks, and flew off northward.

Wien planned to return that same day, May 14. Merrill's log outlines what happened:

May 14: Noel Wien . . . did not return although weather fine except for stiff breeze.

May 15: Weather foggy parts of day but good for considerable period in morning. No Noel.

May 16: Low clouds and low visibility or foggy all day. Tried snowshoeing down a runway.

May 17: Low clouds and fog. Snowshoed runway did not harden at all.

May 18: Started to clear runway at 1:15 a.m. Worked until 2 p.m. Others probably 4 hours each. Decided impractical to do.

May 19: Practically clear midnight. Sunset 11:45 rose 1:00 by clock. (15 min. slow). Observations not carefully made. Blowing hard all day. Snow blowing badly.

May 20: Blowing hard all day. Wind ENE as usual. Compass variation seems to be not over 15 degrees E.

May 21: Foggy and blowing snow all day until about 11:00 p.m. Could see north horizon then.

May 22: Cleared some in a.m and more in p.m. Tried to get off but no chance—even alone. No wind. Robertson and Clarke decided to walk for

HE (MERRILL) DOESN'T SAY MUCH, BUT INDICATES THAT OUR SITUATION MAY BE MORE SERIOUS THAN WE ALLOW OURSELVES TO BELIEVE.

— EXCERPTS FROM THE RECOLLECTIONS OF CHARLES CLARKE

Barrow. Would follow course of about 315 degrees Mag. I decided to take my chance with the ship. They left at 11 p.m. Have very little grub. Weather is calm and while overcast is not snowing. According to sun-compass (watch) they went a little east of north. Doubt whether I could make it to Barrow on foot.

The diary of cameraman Charles Clarke adds detail to the story sketched by Merrill in his log:

After Wien's plane had become a diminishing speck in the sky, we got out the emergency rations and had a little meal consisting of bouillon, rice, and a piece of chocolate each. From the first our "meals" were very sparing, as we had only
1 lb. of raisins
5 lbs. of rice
1 lb. of sweet bar chocolate
2 small cans of bouillon cubes
1 can of army emergency rations
3 cups sugar
1 package Rye Crisp
1 dozen tea bags
We had only two meals a day, and towards the last, only one.
The wind was cold and raw, the temperature 18 above. Merrill started to build an ice house, then returned to the plane and cooked some bouillon and raisins for supper. It is light all night here, and at 10 p.m. I got out my movie camera and took some scenes of the stranded plane. No sign of Wien, so crawled in robe to sleep.

As Russel Merrill's Travel Air sat stranded on the arctic plain in May 1928, the annual season of perpetual daylight had returned to the Barrow region. These views of the nighttime sun were taken at Barrow at half-hour intervals on June 21.

May 15: Rested better as I had found softer snow to lie on than last night. Had all my clothes on, fur coat included, so was not cold. Arose and got some ice to melt for a little breakfast that Merrill prepared on a gasoline stove in his cockpit. We ate the rest of the scorched rice and raisins left from yesterday, which tasted great. Spent the rest of the day completing the snow house. Dug it down to solid ice of the lake and used the blocks of snow for sides and top. The house was about 2½ feet wide and 8½ feet long, with an arched roof about 4 feet high which allowed one to sit up

MERRILL COOKED THE

SQUIRREL FOR BREAKFAST;

IT HAD A SMELL OF RAT

ABOUT IT, BUT THIS WAS NOT

TIME OR PLACE TO BE FUSSY,

SO WE DOVE IN, AND IT

WASN'T BAD.

— EXCERPTS FROM THE
RECOLLECTIONS OF
CHARLES CLARKE

inside. I got the bag of fur costumes we had brought and laid them on the floor to sit on, because the heat from the body melts the ice and you are lucky if you have only frozen trousers.

7 p.m.: No possibility of help tonight. So busy all day. I didn't notice we are apparently stranded out here in nowhere, but the plane with its drooping flippers does remind me of a broken bird. Merrill is heating some water for tea—anything hot! Merrill and I both tried to sleep in the ice house, end to end, but after three hours he went back to his cockpit. He doesn't say much, but indicates that our situation may be more serious than we allow ourselves to believe.

May 16: Cloudy but no wind, comparatively warm. We have given up hope of Wien flying back or dog teams finding us; if possible they would have been here by this time. Perhaps something happened to Hart and Wien and they never made Barrow. Our only hope now is a clear day and wind to help us get off.

Went for a long walk around south bank of the lake, and saw caribou tracks; if we had been able to get one we would have had plenty to eat. Saw something sitting up on the bank like a rabbit, so borrowed Merrill's .22 hoping to get some meat. Found it to be a spermophile or arctic squirrel, but as I shot he ducked down the hole. After returning to the plane, a squirrel came sniffing up and I had better luck, so I skinned him and cut up the meat to soak for further use. It was poor, just out of hibernation and full of fleas. . . .

May 17: Before rising I could hear wind blowing and thought my prayers were answered. My shoes were frozen stiff, and I had to put them in the robe with me to soften them. Outside, I was disappointed—foggy all about and no chance to get away. Very cold and disagreeable too. Merrill cooked the squirrel for breakfast; it had a smell of rat about it, but this was not time or place to be fussy, so we dove in, and it wasn't bad.

I have been in the cabin all day with Robertson. We've been miserable because we can't turn around. The cabin is loaded with camera equipment and we have to lie over the sharp corners of the camera cases. . . .

May 18: On arising, a stiff cold breeze was blowing and Merrill was cutting away the snow in front of the plane to make a runway, so Captain [Robertson] and I pitched in and helped. All we had to work with was an axe and a pair of snowshoes which we used as shovels. We worked for four hours and had removed about a ton of ice, but the wind increased and it began to snow and filled in the runway faster than we could clean it out, so we gave it up and went into the cabin, trying to be cheerful in spite of the way things were turning out. Merrill and I hung the robes and the skins on the struts to dry; the robe was solidly frozen and dangerous to sleep on, so I spent the night in the cabin. It was now 40 above zero.

May 19: Still snowing and very cold. The cabin is now frost-lined and snow is filling in through every crack; every fixed thing is covered with lint-like snow, and we had to clean it out carefully to save the remaining robe and equipment. Merrill slept in the cockpit. We are getting used to it now—the fatigued body is not so particular.

May 20: The storm is still on, and it is blowing continually. We have been here seven days. We sang songs and joked.

May 21: Storm still on. Beginning to feel the lack of food. My stomach twists and contracts as though to turn each fold and crevice inside-out. It is becoming difficult to rest, too. We sat up most of the night watching the sun travel behind the broken clouds to the north. We retired expecting to find it clear in the morning, and in a more cheerful frame of mind.

THE STORM IS STILL ON, AND IT IS BLOWING CONTINUALLY. WE HAVE BEEN HERE SEVEN DAYS. WE SANG SONGS AND JOKED.

— EXCERPTS FROM THE RECOLLECTIONS OF CHARLES CLARKE

May 22: Awakened by the sound of wings creaking. The wind had stopped and a thaw had set in. Water dripping from icicles on the plane and the frost melting inside. When blue sky appeared in the southwest, and north over Barrow, we unloaded all the camera equipment and piled it on the lake, marking it by a black flag (changing bag) tied to the leg of the tripod. The only weight in the plane was our bag of clothes. We then cleared the snow from in front of the plane, and after starting the motor, with great effort we got it clear of drifts onto firmer snow. But the plane, sinking in too deeply in the new-fallen snow, would not move forward.

We all decided it was useless to remain any longer, as we were becoming weaker from lack of food as each day passed. So Captain and I decided to walk to Barrow, which we estimated was 60 miles northwest of us. In the event that a clear day combination came up, Russel would try to get the plane off and pick us up. If not, we were to send back help by dog team along our trail. We are going to hold a course of 315 Magnetic, west of north. Russel is cooking up some rice now—the only food we have had today save a piece of chocolate about an inch square. After that Captain and I will set out to take advantage of the calm night.

It is now 9:15 p.m. Russel put in the rest of the squirrel to flavor the rice, and when it was done he passed the whole to us, saying that was our share. He said that he had to fix something about the plane; but we knew he had not taken any for himself, so we divided it up and saw to it that he ate his share.

After this, we checked over the remaining food, which consisted of a little uncooked rice, tea, and a few spoonsful of sugar, ½ pound of raisins, ½ pound of Rye Crisp, and a 1-pound can of army rations—a bar chocolate compound. As we would be unable to cook en route, and Russel could, he

Unable to move his plane in the deep snow on the frozen lake where he was forced down, Russell Merrill tied it down and finally left to hike for Barrow on May 24, 1928. He had been stranded for eleven days with little food and no signs of help. His passengers had left two days earlier to attempt the trek to Barrow.

took the rice, tea, sugar, and we took the other rations. About 11 we started out; when we were at the crest of the ridge, we waved our last goodbye to Russel and plunged off into the bleak waste ahead.

Russell Merrill was now alone. His logbook tells how he finally decided that he, too, must set off on foot across the snow-covered arctic tundra:

May 23: Cleared about 30 ft. in front of ship. Foggy in morning (after 3) but cleared some in p.m. Before I got drifted snow from runway, wind changed and it became foggy. Found doughnut in tail of ship! Will probably cook all rice and hit the trail myself.

May 24: Flying conditions 1 a.m. seemed favorable so tried to take off in spite of no wind. Nosed her up, bending propeller. Pulled her tail down, tied her down, drained oil. No damage whatever except to prop. Leaving at 9:45 p.m. Wearing Robertson's fur-lined jacket and undershirt of Clarke's. Also taking Clarke's sleeping bag and a Thermos bottle—owner unknown. Will follow compass course of 315 degrees (Mag.) unless same proves to be too far from true north. Will follow this until I reach river going in approximately same direction and will follow river to coast. Have enough rice cooked with me to last four days anyway. Hope to make Barrow or a native home, but rather doubt whether I can. Dearest love to my wife, boys and two fine brothers.

R. H. Merrill

Chapter Eleven

TREK TO BARROW

BACK IN ANCHORAGE, PEOPLE BEGAN TO

WORRY. THE EXPECTED MESSAGE FROM

MERRILL, REPORTING HIS SAFE RETURN FROM

BARROW TO FAIRBANKS, DID NOT ARRIVE.

AFTER **N**OEL **W**IEN FLEW OFF FOR HELP ON **M**AY 14, 1928, LEAVING **R**USSEL **M**ERRILL AND THE OTHER TWO MEN AT THE FROZEN LAKE, HE CIRCLED UNTIL HE FOUND A TRAIL THAT LED HIM TO **B**ARROW. **H**E REFUELED AT **B**ARROW AND TOOK OFF AT ONCE, HEADING SOUTHEAST. **B**UT A STRONG CROSSWIND WAS BLOWING, AND DRIFTING SNOW OBSCURED THE ROUTE HE HAD FLOWN AND SO CAREFULLY NOTED A FEW HOURS BEFORE.

Wien flew a circular search pattern under low clouds that limited his visual range. His fuel ran low, and with no sign of Merrill's Travel Air, Wien returned to Barrow.

For the next six days a blizzard raged. Searching was out of the question. Wien fumed and worried about Merrill and his passengers, down on the tundra and probably in the thick of the storm. Wien found an old pair of airplane skis, left in Barrow that spring by the Wilkins Arctic Expedition. While waiting out the storm, he repaired the skis and fitted them to the Stinson in place of its wheels.

As soon as the blizzard slackened, Wien took off with Virgil Hart. The landscape was a blur of white from horizon to horizon, with no landmarks to guide him. Every trace of life was buried beneath two feet of newly fallen snow. Forced down at a reindeer camp, the men were held up by bad weather for four days. It was now twelve days since they had left the Travel Air and its three occupants, hoping to return that same day.

Back in Anchorage, people began to worry. The expected message from Merrill, reporting his safe return to Fairbanks after delivering the Fox party to Barrow, did not arrive. They knew that Barrow had no wireless and that

Overleaf: On the eighth day of his survival trek toward Barrow, Russel Merrill reached what he believed to be the ice-covered Arctic Ocean. But he couldn't be certain, because the flat, frozen surface blended into the tundra with no visible break. The scene would have looked much like this scene of the Arctic Ocean at Barrow, taken about July 1, 1928.

The wheels on Noel Wien's Stinson were changed for skis at Barrow. Hampered by poor weather, Wien was searching anxiously for the airplane that was stranded on a frozen arctic lake with Russel Merrill and two passengers.

Merrill and Wien might have been delayed by bad weather. But at least one of the planes should have made it to Fairbanks to send a message.

On May 24—the day Merrill left his airplane to trek to Barrow—it was decided that Anchorage Air Transport's other pilot, Matt Nieminen, would fly north in *Anchorage No. 2* to investigate. Private Richard Heyser of the U.S. Signal Corps came along with his radio equipment—including a 27-foot aerial mast that they strapped onto the plane.

Nieminen flew to Barrow from Fairbanks by the longer but safer route

THE TWO PILOTS SPOTTED

MERRILL'S *ANCHORAGE NO. 1*

HALF-BURIED IN

SNOWDRIFTS. THERE WAS

NO SIGN OF LIFE.

around the Endicott Mountains, stopping at Ruby, Kotzebue (overnight), and Wainwright. At Barrow, he learned that Wien had reached there safely with Virgil Hart and was out searching for Merrill and the others. He was told that dog teams also had joined the search.

Wien returned to Barrow two days later to find Nieminen ready to join him in the air search. They changed the tires on *Anchorage No. 2*, installing the larger tires from Wien's plane that had been replaced by skis. On June 1, Wien and Nieminen took off at the same time, with Hart and Heyser as extra pairs of eyes. After flying east along the coast for an hour, they turned and flew south for nearly another hour.

Suddenly there it was. Nieminen saw *Anchorage No. 1* half-buried in snowdrifts. The two planes circled overhead. There was no sign of life. A black flag drooped from a tripod in the snow. Both pilots landed near Merrill's plane. Nieminen's craft nosed over in the deep snow, but without damage. Merrill's plane, in good shape except for a bent propeller, was tied down by ropes anchored in holes in the solid lake ice.

Merrill's logbook, found in the cockpit map pocket, told the searchers about the trek to Barrow undertaken by Charles Clarke and Jack Robertson and, later, by Merrill.

Wien and Nieminen flew off immediately. Wien headed straight for the camp of trapper John Hegness, whose cabin was located at Halkett, 125 miles southeast along the coast from Barrow and not far from the lake where Merrill had landed *Anchorage No. 1*. Hegness agreed to join the search.

Nieminen, meanwhile, selected a course that followed the route Merrill and his passengers were likely to have taken in hiking to Barrow. He found an old dog team trail that at one point was crossed by fresh tracks of men on foot. He followed the tracks down the coast to an igloo, where he landed and

found signs that Clarke and Robertson had stayed overnight. Nieminen took off and headed in the direction the men would have taken toward Barrow.

Soon he saw two men below him at a point about fifty miles from Barrow. At first he thought they were natives; one was wearing a full-length fur outfit. When Nieminen dropped closer, he realized it was Clarke and Robertson; the fur was part of the Fox Film Expedition gear. Russel Merrill was still alone out there somewhere on the tundra.

Nieminen landed on a sand spit and bundled the two exhausted and

Jack Robertson (left) and Charles Clarke were rescued June 1, 1928, by Matt Nieminen flying *Anchorage No. 2.* The exhausted, starving men had been hiking from their stranded plane for ten days. Clarke lost forty pounds, Robertson thirty.

half-starved men into his plane. Heyser gave up his seat and was left on the beach with his radio equipment (which turned out to be of little value in the search efforts because of technical problems). Nieminen flew to Barrow with the weak, frostbitten, sunburned men. Clarke had lost forty pounds and Robertson thirty. Clarke was badly crippled with a torn tendon in his leg, and Robertson had lost half-a-dozen toenails from frostbite.

More dog teams were dispatched from Barrow in the direction of Smith Bay on the theory that Merrill might have taken that route. Nieminen and Wien serviced their planes that afternoon in Barrow and set out to search the area to the east and southeast. They flew low, hoping Merrill would be able to hear the sounds of their motors and signal to them.

When Merrill set out on foot May 24 from the downed plane, his food supply consisted of some cooked rice that he said, in his logbook, would be enough for at least four days. But the rice actually consisted of only a few spoonfuls, which he had cooked in a tin cup, with some snow, on the oil stove in the cockpit. Smoke from the stove covered the outside of the cup with a thick layer of black soot, which he purposely did not clean off because he knew the blackened exterior would absorb the sun's heat to help in melting snow in the cup.

Merrill began his trek to Barrow just before 10 p.m., but the weight and bulk of the sleeping bag he was packing soon proved too much of a hindrance. He returned it to the plane, even though it cost him a critical couple of hours of hiking time. Because the bag was valuable and belonged to someone else, he felt he had no right to discard it.

He started out again at midnight, using his watch to guide him. By observing the angle of the sun to the horizon, and knowing the time of day from his watch, he could estimate a compass course. On the featureless, flat, white tundra, distances were difficult to reckon. The white glare threw everything out of perspective. Merrill could see what he thought were mountains, only to find out later that they were small, nearby ice ridges.

He trudged on as fast as he could. The snow was thin-crusted, which made for hard walking. From time to time he had to lie down, but he didn't dare rest long. Each time he felt sleepy, he would force himself to get to his feet and move on before he got too cold. After several days of walking, he knew he must be near the coastline.

During the sunny hours of the day he would put snow in the cup of rice. The sun would heat the dark, sooty outside surface of the cup and cause the snow to melt, creating a watery gruel from the already-cooked rice. He would drink the fluid off but leave the rice itself.

As he fought his way through the snow one day, he suddenly noticed something moving—then a number of things moving. Were his eyes deceiving him? He stopped, and sure enough, small animals were running across the crust of the snow. After a while, he realized they were lemmings, small rodents of the Arctic that periodically migrate to the sea to end their short lives.

Merrill found a lemming burrow, curled up in the snow nearby, and waited. He dozed for a while but awakened when lemmings began scooting about near him. He shot one with his .22-caliber automatic pistol. Since there was no vegetation to burn for a fire, he skinned the animal and ate the hindquarters raw. After that he shot as many lemmings as he could to supplement the rice gruel.

On his eighth day on foot, Merrill came to what he believed was the Arctic Ocean. It was impossible to be certain; the flat, frozen surface that

MERRILL SHOT ONE OF THE LEMMINGS WITH HIS .22-CALIBER AUTOMATIC PISTOL. SINCE THERE WAS NO VEGETATION TO BURN FOR A FIRE, HE SKINNED THE ANIMAL AND ATE THE HINDQUARTERS RAW. AFTER THAT HE SHOT AS MANY LEMMINGS AS HE COULD TO SUPPLEMENT THE RICE GRUEL.

MERRILL FOUND AN OLD

CACHE OF WHALE MEAT,

PROBABLY LEFT BY ESKIMOS

FOR DOG FOOD. THE MEAT

WAS DECAYED AND SMELLED

RANCID, BUT IT TASTED

WONDERFUL TO HIM.

might have been ocean ice blended into the tundra with no visible break. There he found an old cache of whale meat, probably left by Eskimos for dog food. The meat was decayed and smelled rancid, but it tasted wonderful to him. He pushed on but began to feel so weak that he turned back for more of the whale meat. He hated to retrace his steps, but he needed the food.

Twice on his walk back to the meat cache, Merrill heard the drone of an aircraft overhead, a marvelous sound in that eerily noiseless land. He stopped and waved until he was exhausted. Both times the plane flew directly overhead, but the pilot didn't see him. It was encouraging to know someone was searching for him, but disheartening to see the pilot fly past. After that it was even harder to keep plodding ahead.

A threat more lethal than the pangs of hunger soon confronted him. His eyes were dimming with snowblindness. The surfaces of his eyes stung, and his field of vision narrowed and darkened. He tried to be sensible. He would figure something out. He lay down to rest and think.

Then he heard a sound in the distance, a faint creaking—like a dog harness under strain. Soon came the unmistakable whine of sled runners on packed snow. And finally the panting of dogs.

Raising himself on an elbow, he called to the musher: "What are the chances of bumming a ride to Barrow?"

"Sorry," a voice replied, "but I've got a full load."

Merrill rose to his feet and began to move in the sled tracks, trying to follow. The musher halted his dogs and came back to him.

It was trapper John Hegness, who had been so moved by the pitiful figure lying in the snow that he could only respond to Merrill's wry request with his own grim humor.

Hegness told Merrill that he had, in fact, seen him from a distance through field glasses and at first thought he was a polar bear. It was June 4—eleven days since Merrill had set out on foot from the airplane and three weeks since he had landed on the frozen lake. Hegness heated some soup and spooned it into Merrill. He bundled him into blankets inside the sled so he could rush him to food, warmth, and medical attention at Barrow, still forty miles away.

When Hegness found Merrill, he still carried his blackened tin cup of rice. Merrill said he was saving it for an emergency.

Two days of fog at Barrow had grounded the search planes of Noel Wien and Matt Nieminen. On the morning of June 4, they were warming up their motors to resume the search when John Hegness appeared. On his sled lay the still figure of a man. Wien and Nieminen instantly knew it was Russel Merrill. The few minutes between the time the sled first came into sight and the moment it was close enough that they could see Merrill was still alive "were about the most harrowing any of us had ever gone through," Nieminen said.

Merrill was taken to the hospital at Barrow, where he was treated for snowblindness and malnutrition. He and the medical staff felt that bed rest would cure what appeared to be, more than anything else, a simple case of exhaustion. Though very weak, Merrill felt well enough to get out of bed after the third day at the hospital. He insisted upon accompanying Wien to the lake to retrieve *Anchorage No. 1.* He was afraid the plane would break through the melting ice on the lake and be lost.

Their first attempt to find the plane, on June 7, was abandoned when the motor on Wien's Stinson malfunctioned. They tried again June 11, flying for more than five hours, eyes glued to the white wastes, only to realize

Trapper John Hegness arrives at Barrow on June 4, 1928, bearing the still figure of Russel Merrill in the front dogsled. Merrill—malnourished and snow blind—was found eleven days after setting off on foot from his downed airplane. It had been three weeks since he made the forced landing on a frozen arctic lake.

that wind and snow had buried every trail. Exhausted, Merrill returned to his hospital bed.

Two days later Wien took Nieminen with him and found Merrill's plane. They bolted on a new propeller, and Nieminen flew the plane to Barrow. Merrill wanted to fly the plane home right then and there, but the other pilots insisted he didn't have the energy to undertake a long flight. Sure enough, by the next day Merrill was running a high fever. The initial diagnosis was typhoid, the result of eating lemmings that were almost certainly diseased and, possibly, the rotten whale meat.

Robertson and Clarke recovered from their ordeal after a week in the Barrow hospital. By then the whaling season was over, the snow was melting, and the Fox Film team was resigned to heading south empty-handed. Clarke decided to return to California. Robertson planned to travel to Wainwright, where he would help Fox director Ewing Scott film whales.

A dinner, featuring wild goose, was held to celebrate the rescues and to bid farewell to the Fox Film team. Merrill was there, a fugitive from the heavy meats, powdered eggs, and canned milk that constituted hospital food in Barrow. He had eaten no fresh veg-

Pilot Matt Nieminen (left) found Jack Robertson and Charles Clarke as the exhausted men trekked across the arctic plain. Trapper John Hegness (right), traveling by dogsled, rescued Russel Merrill when he found the snow-blind aviator lying in the snow forty miles from the safety of Barrow.

etables or milk since leaving Wiseman a month before. But the banquet's offerings were too much for his starved digestive system and probably prolonged his illness.

On June 14, Noel Wien in his Stinson and Matt Nieminen in *Anchorage No. 2* left for Fairbanks and Anchorage, respectively. Merrill stayed at the hospital, too sick to move. It was becoming clear that he was in grave condition. At the beginning of July word came to Anchorage Air Transport from Barrow that Merrill was worse and needed to be moved to better facilities.

Wien flew north with his novice-pilot brother Ralph as a passenger. They wrapped Merrill in a fur sleeping bag and gently placed him on the floor of Wien's cabin Stinson. Accompanied by a trained nurse, Emily Morgan, they headed for home the long way—via Wainwright, Kotzebue, and Nome— with Ralph Wien flying *Anchorage No. 1*. The attending physician at each stop had his own theory about the strange fever that was wasting Merrill. At Nome he was placed in the hospital for observation and treatment, and a week of bad weather further held the rescue mission there until July 21.

After leaving Nome, a heavy rainstorm forced them down at Kaltag. Merrill, too weak to be moved, spent twenty-one hours in the plane at Kaltag under the constant attention of Nurse Morgan as rain pelted in and mosquitoes made the situation even worse. Merrill was blue around the eyes and mouth from exposure and fever. The next day the plane reached Fairbanks, where he was hospitalized.

Thyra Merrill hurried north to Fairbanks to meet her husband. She steeled herself for the shock of seeing him after his two months of suffering. But in spite of her mental preparation, she was shaken. The pallor of his skin was a hospital white, his brown hair had turned gray, his voice was hollow and without tone. Her husband, strong and healthy when he left Anchorage in

A crowd watches on July 26, 1928, as Russel Merrill is lifted from
Anchorage No. 1 after he was flown from Fairbanks to Anchorage. Merrill
was still suffering the serious effects of his attempted trek to Barrow
from his downed airplane.

mid-May, looked old and frail. But within the battered, weakened frame was a glow Thyra recognized. When she saw the life that still shone in his eyes, she knew he would be fine.

A few days in Fairbanks brought enough improvement for doctors to authorize a move to Anchorage. Thyra sat in the nurse's place on July 26 for what turned out to be a rough flight, but Russel seemed not to mind. He continually asked for food, a good sign. Between doses of medicine, she fed him sandwiches and cream.

Thyra was worried about the effect Russel's appearance would have on their sons, Dick and Bob. "But when we brought Russel into the house on the stretcher," she recalled, "they seemed to know at once that he was all right."

CHAPTER TWELVE
CHANGES: 1929

RUSSEL MERRILL'S RECOVERY WAS SLOW, PARTLY BECAUSE HE WAS A REST-LESS PATIENT. THROUGHOUT AUGUST 1928 HE WAS BEDRIDDEN, TOO WEAK TO MOVE EVEN AFTER THE FEVER HAD BURNED ITSELF OUT. HIS CONDITION WAS FI-NALLY THOUGHT TO BE NOT TYPHOID, BUT TULAREMIA OR ROCKY MOUNTAIN SPOTTED FEVER, AILMENTS THAT CAN LAST AS LONG AS SIX MONTHS BUT ARE SELDOM FATAL.

Then, slowly and almost imperceptibly at first, his strength began to return. From the moment he was able to concentrate for any length of time, he was busy planning his return to flying. He began to read as soon as his hands could hold reading material, poring over aviation literature for hours at a time, learning what the state of the art was. Another tonic for Merrill was finding that he was the only Alaska airman listed in the 1928 edition of *Who's Who in American Aeronautics*, the blue book of aviation in the United States.

Merrill's convalescence was a watershed in his life. For once, he had time to survey the overall aviation picture from an engineer's point of view, with an experienced pilot's insight. His fertile mind, freed from the constant need to meet schedules and improvise routes, focused on some of the recurring problems he had experienced as a bush pilot.

It never entered his mind that he might give up flying altogether and return to a business career. Nor did it occur to Thyra to urge him to do so. He did plan to go eventually into the entrepreneurial side of aviation, but for now actual flying was still the great direction in his life. As long as he could be of service to this new land, Thyra was fully in accord with his ambitions. She felt that this supportive attitude was almost universal among the wives

Overleaf: *Anchorage No. 1*, piloted by Russel Merrill, was the first plane to land at the new 200-by-1,200-foot airfield in Curry, along the railroad line between Anchorage and Fairbanks. Merrill picked up a Mr. Cummings, manager of the Curry hotel, on December 1, 1928, to fly him to Anchorage.

and mothers of pilots.

One happy outcome of his experience at Barrow was the opportunity to be at home with his family for more than a few days at a time. All pilots resign themselves to absences from home, but Merrill was away for months at a time during the Candle, Lockanok, and Barrow trips. He took advantage of his convalescence to explain to his young boys the intricacies of airplanes and tell them the stories of his flights.

Dick, at age six, loved the sensation of being in the air. Four-year-old Bob was particularly keen on planes. He already knew many parts of a plane and motor. When Russel recovered enough to visit the Anchorage Air Transport hangar in mid-September, Bob went with him. Alonzo Cope allowed him to play around the machines, and before long the drive to the airfield, with Bob along to "help Cope with the planes," became a daily ritual. Bob was in the front cockpit when Russel made an aerobatics flight after his recovery, and as the plane rolled and spun, Bob was delighted. He had complete confidence in his father. Bob would qualify as a naval aviator during World War II.

Merrill resumed flying on September 20 and made his first commercial flight six days later. He was, once again, AAT's only pilot. Matt Nieminen had been taking care of business out of Anchorage between flights to Barrow, but he had left the company August 25 to accept an attractive offer to become executive pilot of Texas Pipeline Company, flying a fast new Lockheed Vega monoplane.

Meanwhile, business was booming as America reached the peak of its post-World War I prosperity. Big-game hunters were becoming an important source of revenue for AAT, just as businessman Gus Gelles had foreseen. AAT offered a complete service to hunting parties, with Merrill ferrying

MERRILL'S CONVALESCENCE WAS A WATERSHED IN HIS LIFE. FOR ONCE, HE HAD TIME TO SURVEY THE OVERALL AVIATION PICTURE FROM AN ENGINEER'S POINT OF VIEW, WITH AN EXPERIENCED PILOT'S INSIGHT.

them to prime areas, making air drops of supplies, and returning the hunters to base. Large animal trophies would be tied to the plane. President Calvin Coolidge's son and a friend flew with Merrill on their hunting trip. At the onset of winter, the passengers tended to be professional outdoorsmen—trappers and fur buyers.

Merrill still made unusual and unexpected flights. He rescued a woman and her infant from Sleetmute, flying back across the Mount Spurr region to Anchorage at midnight. He piloted a honeymoon flight from Akiak to Bethel, breaking through the Kuskokwim River ice on landing, but with no damage to passengers and little to the machine. After witnessing the marriage, he returned to the river and winched the plane out of the water.

Merrill never missed an opportunity to publicize the extraordinary precautions Alaska aviators took to ensure the survival of themselves and their passengers in emergencies, such as the one he and his two passengers endured on their May 1928 flight to Barrow. Merrill had responded back in October 1927 to an inquiry from the Prudential Insurance Company of New York, which was investigating the hazards of aviation: "Alaska boasts a record of no deaths to passengers or pilots of any aircraft in the Territory. A newspaper reporter at Fairbanks once walked into a propeller at Fairbanks and was killed, but this is the only death directly or indirectly chargeable to aviation up here, as far as I know." Thanks to Merrill's safe return from his ordeal at Barrow, this impressive claim was still valid.

The Aeronautics Branch of the Department of Commerce, given responsibility for regulating aviation, asked AAT what safety equipment it provided for its planes. The agency was aware that Merrill and AAT had recently become experts on arctic survival. Merrill's reply of February 16, 1929, said

AAT planes carried 120 pounds of emergency equipment, including the following items:

Large canvas hood for use in warming motor
Stove for warming motor and cooking
10 pounds concentrated food
Cooking utensils
Spare motor parts
Tool kit
Snowshoes, one pair
One gallon lubricating oil
Gasoline funnel with chamois (for filter)
Oil funnel
One five-gallon can for draining motor oil
Matches in sealed container
A .22 long-rifle automatic pistol and ammunition
Axe
Two pocket compasses
Snow glasses
First aid kit
Pyrene
One parka
Cockpit cover
A few miscellaneous items

Merrill noted in his letter: "We have not carried a rifle, as it weighs quite a bit, and it is pretty heavy to carry in case one has to walk. Your suggestion of a Very [flare] pistol seems very good to me and we will either order one or use railroad flares that are available locally. I had the pleasure of the ten-day walk you speak of [Merrill's survival trek for Barrow], and twice during that time I could have stopped passing airplanes if I had had suitable signaling devices."

By April 1929, Anchorage Air Transport had been down to a single pilot, Merrill, for seven months. Another experienced pilot from the States, Frank Dorbandt, arrived in Anchorage April 1, flew a check flight, and was hired. Dorbandt was generous, impulsive, but occasionally hot-tempered, a personality that contrasted with Merrill's. Dorbandt stayed with AAT until mid-July, when he left to become Wien Alaska Airway's Nome-based operator, flying newer aircraft than AAT's Travel Airs.

One of Merrill's first post-recovery projects was to tackle the problem of having proper landing gear for the constantly changing airfield conditions, especially during the spring breakup of ice. Conditions changed overnight. On the return flight from Nome after the 1927 crash-landing near Candle, pilot Ed Young found himself operating the ski-equipped *Anchorage No. 1* on melting river ice, barely a step ahead of the thaw. More recently, the Fox Film Expedition flight to Barrow faced the risk that the planes, on wheels for bare-land operations, would be forced down in the snowfields en route. Of course, this is just what happened. Anchorage Air Transport needed something in the way of all-weather landing gear.

Merrill and Cope decided to combine wheels and skis so aircraft could operate from either snow-covered or cleared airfields, or from fields partially covered with snow. They first mounted wheels outside the skis on *Anchorage No. 1*, the larger plane. Merrill tried this combination April 17 on snow at Lake Spenard at Anchorage. It worked reasonably well, causing

very little drag in the snow.

Then they came up with a better rig, which they called "skeels." It placed the stress of landing where it belongs by setting the wheels in a cutout on the centerline of the skis, giving both wheel and ski the same track. A fairing was fitted over the wheels to reduce drag in the air and keep out snow and ice on the ground.

Cope had the skeels fabricated in the railroad shops, and Merrill tested them during two flights May 1. They worked well, and Merrill used them on a number of flights during the spring of 1929. Another set of skeels was mounted on *Anchorage No. 2.* Similar devices have been developed since, but these skeels were probably the first of their kind.

Alonzo Cope shows off the newly installed "skeels" on *Anchorage No. 2* at the Anchorage airfield in 1929. Cope and Russel Merrill developed the wheel-ski combination that allowed them to take off and land on either snow or bare ground.

Merrill's next safety-related project was installation of a turn-and-bank indicator in *Anchorage No. 1*. This instrument shows the aircraft's rate of turn in a bank when the pilot can see neither the horizon nor the ground. It is also an aid in holding a heading in those conditions. Merrill installed it May 11 and then successfully flew with his head in the cockpit for fifteen minutes—longer than he could maintain straight and level flight in fog or clouds without the help of the indicator.

Big changes were on the horizon for aviation in Anchorage and in the whole of Alaska. On May 4, Ben Eielson returned to Alaska on a mission that promised to further Merrill's goal of expanding airline service in the Territory. Eielson had been in Antarctica with Sir Hubert Wilkins, who was knighted for the trans-Arctic flight made by the two men from Barrow to Spitsbergen, Norway, in mid-April 1928. They followed up that historic achievement by making the first flight over Antarctica, on November 16, 1928. Eielson, now world-famous, returned to Alaska with the solid backing of eastern capital to create an Alaska-wide air service.

Eielson briefed Merrill on his plans for the new service. Eielson would be vice president and general manager, with headquarters in Fairbanks. He would like Merrill to be manager of the Anchorage base, which would be greatly enlarged. Two new pilots would be hired. First, though, negotiations with Anchorage Air Transport and other existing companies would have to be carried out before any changes could be made.

During this period, the burgeoning number of flights in and out of Anchorage made it obvious the town needed a proper airport. This wasn't a project that Anchorage Air Transport could handle by itself. On May 20, Merrill was joined by a prominent Anchorage citizen, Harry Staser, in urg-

BEN EIELSON RETURNED TO

ALASKA ON A MISSION THAT

PROMISED TO FURTHER

MERRILL'S GOAL OF

EXPANDING AIRLINE SERVICE

IN THE TERRITORY.

ing the Anchorage City Council to support construction of a multi-runway airport. The Chamber of Commerce backed the request. The council established the Anchorage Aeronautical Commission and gave it political weight by naming Mayor Oscar Gill as chairman.

The commission reported back favorably on the proposal for a new airport. The city council voted to spend $2,000 toward the project, to be matched by the Territorial Board of Road Commissioners. A level site of thirty-five acres one mile east of the city was selected. On July 10, the road commission contracted for clearing of brush for two 2,000-foot intersecting runways, followed by contracts for ploughing and grading. Work on the new airfield was completed August 22, 1929.

The new facility was named Anchorage Aviation Field (later renamed Anchorage Municipal Airport). In 1929 it had no buildings, no hangars, no fueling equipment—nothing but two dirt-and-gravel runways and a wind cone.

Russel Merrill finally decided to take a holiday. He had been pushing hard throughout 1929—often making three round-trip flights in a day, helping Alonzo Cope develop the skeels, experimenting with blind-flying techniques, giving advice to the Aeronautics Branch of the Department of Commerce, and pondering the future of airlines in Alaska and his role in developing them. So in early August he and Thyra joined two other couples on an automobile tour of the Richardson Highway.

Like travel almost anywhere in Alaska, the tour of the Richardson Highway was not simply a matter of packing a picnic basket, gassing up the Franklin, and unfolding a road map. The travelers started by shipping their two cars, a Franklin and a Buick, by train to Seward, then by boat to Valdez. At that time, there was no road connection to the highway from Anchorage.

The voyage from Seward to Valdez was a scheduled twelve-hour trip, but it took two and a half days with stops at canneries to load fish.

From Valdez, they drove north across the Chugach Mountains. Beyond the mountains they forded several glacial streams where parts of the highway or its rudimentary bridges had washed out. During one of these plunges into rushing waters, one car struck a submerged rock and broke its rear axle. The six vacationers dragged the car up onto the bank, left most of their luggage in the damaged car, and took off in the remaining vehicle. They arranged with some road workers to return the damaged car to Valdez for shipment to Anchorage while the single crowded vehicle carried on toward Fairbanks.

They spent three days on the highway getting to Fairbanks. Thyra wrote that "it was peaceful, with only the natural woodland sounds, no telephones to bring a demand for service, not even the drone of an airplane. Russel grew relaxed and boyish." At Fairbanks, Ben Eielson and other friends entertained the travelers at the Eighteen Mile House. Then they continued on to Circle, which boasted a commercial hot spring.

Back in Fairbanks once more, Russel had to leave the other five vacationers and catch the train south to resume flying at Anchorage. Thyra wanted to return with him, but Russel persuaded her to make a planned side trip to McKinley Park with the others. While they were in the park, Russel flew over their cabins and blipped his motor three times in greeting. Merrill said later that the auto trip not only offered him a chance to relax, but also gave him a greater appreciation of the magnitude of the land they were knitting together by airplane.

On August 16, Merrill's first day back at work after his vacation, he flew a load of supplies into Pontilla's Lake, 120 miles northeast of Anchorage in

Russel Merrill arrives at Kenai, seventy miles southeast of Anchorage, with a hunting party. The plane is *Anchorage No. 1*, the Travel Air Model CW.

the Rainy Pass district. The next day he flew a second load to the same location, a big-game camp set up by Gus Gelles's Alaska Guides. On August 19, Merrill flew James A. Stillman, former president of the National Bank of New York, and his colleague James H. Durrell into the camp. During their month's stay, Durrell's log recorded that he personally saw 560 caribou, 154 white sheep, 97 moose, 104 bears, and 4 wolverines.

Russel Merrill prepares to fly hunters James H. Durrell and James A. Stillman from the Cook Inlet mud flats to a lake in the Rainy Pass area on August 19, 1929. It was the last day of operation for Anchorage Air Transport, which was bought out by the new Alaska-wide air service, Alaskan Airways.

These mid-August flights were Merrill's last for Anchorage Air Transport. In August the new company for which Ben Eielson had been acting as agent—Alaskan Airways, Inc.—officially took over most of the independent outfits, including AAT, Wien Alaska Airways, and Bennett-Rodebaugh Company.

Alaskan Airways offered $25,000 cash for AAT, and the company's shareholders readily voted to accept. Each recovered his investment with interest. Preferred stockholders, who had come into the company when it was first formed and when funds were urgently needed, doubled their money—a good return considering that despite $37,000 in revenues during 1928, AAT had experienced setbacks and had drawn heavily on its capital.

While AAT's aircraft had been damaged several times during the life of the company, there had been no serious injuries or fatalities. As its days as an independent enterprise drew to a close, Anchorage Air Transport could point to its pioneering achievements in aviation and to a safety record that was outstanding for one of the most hazardous flying environments in the world. At midnight on August 19, Anchorage Air Transport ceased to exist.

Merrill kept busy with the new company. Among his first jobs was flying big-bear hunter Butler Greer, president of the Bankers Utilities Company of San Francisco, into Two Lakes, just west of Merrill Pass. Greer and other hunters had great success in 1929, helping Anchorage become the hub of big-game hunting in Alaska. Anchorage aviation now had a loyal and widespread customer base of hunters, miners, fishermen, trappers, and general travelers.

Aviation in the Anchorage area had evolved, and Russel Merrill was the engine of its evolution. Merrill's spirit of exploration, his discovery of new routes, his zeal for safe flying, and his impressive flight record had turned a risky pioneering venture into the reality of dependable commercial aviation.

AS ITS DAYS AS AN INDEPENDENT ENTERPRISE DREW TO A CLOSE, ANCHORAGE AIR TRANSPORT COULD POINT TO ITS PIONEERING ACHIEVEMENTS IN AVIATION AND TO A SAFETY RECORD THAT WAS OUTSTANDING FOR ONE OF THE MOST HAZARDOUS FLYING ENVIRONMENTS IN THE WORLD.

Russel and Thyra Merrill pose with their sons Dick, age 6, and Bob, age 4, in 1929. The picture was taken in a house they were renting at 920 W. Sixth Street (now Sixth Avenue) in Anchorage. The house stands largely unaltered today.

CHAPTER THIRTEEN

HAVING PIONEERED

"I'M SORRY I CAN'T STAY FOR THE BIG PARTY,
BOYS," RUSSEL SAID AS HIS TWO YOUNG SONS
CLIMBED UP FOR A GOODBYE KISS.

"SEPTEMBER 15, 1929. IT WAS BOB'S FIFTH BIRTHDAY, AND HE WAS FEELING PRETTY GROWN-UP," READS AN EXCERPT FROM THYRA MERRILL'S WRITINGS ABOUT THE MERRILL FAMILY'S LIFE IN ALASKA. IT CONTINUES:

He seemed so much like a little Russel as he walked around in his quiet way; suppressed excitement showed in his eyes while he waited for his first party to begin.

When the doorbell rang, he thought it was Dick coming home from a friend's house and rushed to the door.

"Why, Daddy!" I heard him say. "Are you coming to my party after all?"

I went into the dining room. Russel, both hands filled with sticks of bright balloons, stood by the decorated table smiling down at his small son. He turned to me.

"Thought I'd surprise you with a donation for the party," he said. "Those hunters weren't quite ready, so I had time to run this errand. I have to pick them up at the hotel in a few minutes to make it down to Tustumena Lake and back tonight. Where's Dick?"

Just then Dick came in.

"I'm sorry I can't stay for the big party, boys," Russel said as they climbed up for a goodbye kiss.

That evening, with the celebration over and the happy boys tucked in bed, I went to a movie with some friends. I came home to find Russel working on his logbooks.

"Did you get through?" I asked.

"Yes, but I'll have to take more supplies in to them in the morning."

As hectic as it was, September 16, 1929, was not an unusual day for Russel Merrill. He was the only pilot flying out of Anchorage at a time when the growth in big-game hunting was pushing the Anchorage base to log more mileage and more freight than any other field in the Alaskan Airways operation. He had now been operating for almost a month under the new company that bought out Alaska Air Transport.

Thyra awakened him at 3:00 that morning. He ate his usual breakfast of fruit, three shredded wheat biscuits, four slices of toast, two eggs, and bacon. He took off at 5:30 in *Anchorage No. 1*, on pontoons, with Gus Gelles and a hunting guide to fly down to Tustumena Lake, eighty miles south on the Kenai Peninsula. He returned with Gelles at 9:00 a.m. He immediately loaded supplies, another guide, and Gelles and left for the big-game camp near Rainy Pass, returning at 2:30 p.m., again with Gelles.

Merrill ate lunch before loading a compressor, bound for the New York-Alaska Company's mining operation on Bear Creek at Nyac, near Bethel. The mine was closed down, awaiting the urgently needed equipment. The 235-pound compressor was loaded close to the cabin plane's center of gravity and securely lashed in place. Some fifty pounds of first-class mail that Merrill was carrying to distribute along the way provided movable ballast.

As usual, Merrill had planned for almost any contingency. He wouldn't fly all the way to Nyac that day. He planned to stop for the night at Sleetmute on the Kuskokwim River, three hours from Anchorage. If bad weather kept him from Sleetmute, he would stop overnight at B. F. Greer's camp at Chakachamna Lake or George Shaben's cabin near there. The next day he would fly on to Nyac, then to Bethel to pick up a passenger and some live foxes for a fur farm on the upper Kuskokwim.

Merrill could have waited until the next day, the 17th, to start this long

MERRILL COULD HAVE WAITED UNTIL THE NEXT DAY, SEPTEMBER 17, TO START HIS NEXT LONG TRIP. AFTER ALL, HE HAD BEEN UP SINCE 3:00 A.M. BUT PROVIDING DEPENDABLE AIR SERVICE WAS MERRILL'S TOP PRIORITY, AND MEETING HIS SCHEDULE WAS UPPERMOST IN HIS MIND.

trip. After all, he had been up since 3:00 a.m. and had already made two round-trips that day. But providing dependable air service was Merrill's top priority, and meeting his schedule was uppermost in his mind.

Merrill left Anchorage alone at 4:10 p.m. carrying the compressor and the mail, planning to briefly head south down Cook Inlet before turning west toward the mine. As he took off, the weather was calm, the sky slightly overcast, with medium visibility.

A heavy storm hit Cook Inlet and the surrounding territory beginning at 11 p.m. and continuing for several hours. But friends and family didn't begin to worry until September 18, two days after Merrill left Anchorage for his assignments along the Kuskokwim. Ben Eielson flew down from Fairbanks on the 19th in a new open-cockpit Waco 10 to investigate.

Eielson flew the 225 miles to Sleetmute the next day with Alonzo Cope as his observer. No one had seen Merrill or his plane. Eielson and Cope began a systematic search of the routes Merrill might have taken. He was to have followed the westbound route he had pioneered himself through the Alaska Range, the opening soon to become known as Merrill Pass.

Joe Crosson, one of the most experienced pilots in Alaska and a veteran of the 1928 Wilkins Antarctic Expedition, arrived in Anchorage September 21 on his way to join Alaskan Airways at Fairbanks. He mounted pontoons on the smaller *Anchorage No. 2* and flew off to follow the course Merrill had set for himself. Harvey Barnhill, a new Alaskan Airways pilot, flew a recently assembled three-seat New Standard biplane down from Fairbanks to join the search.

No one felt a sense of panic. Based on Merrill's survival record, everyone assumed he had landed somewhere to make minor repairs to his aircraft or

Russel Merrill takes *Anchorage No. 1* off from Spenard Lake, Anchorage, at 4:10 p.m. on September 16, 1929, on his final flight.

that bad weather had forced him off course.

Eielson and Cope completed a zigzag search from the Kuskokwim to Chakachamna Lake. They dropped notes over Butler Greer's hunting camp at Two Lakes, hoping for information. He had none. Eielson and Crosson scoured the territory from Two Lakes and Merrill Pass to Anchorage a total of four times. Eielson covered more than 3,000 miles in the three days following the 18th, and Crosson duplicated that feat over the next few days. They flew in all kinds of weather; the early Alaskan winter was already upon them.

Next they combed the region surrounding Cook Inlet in case Merrill had found it necessary to land before reaching the mountains on his westward leg. The tide was in when he left Anchorage; the plane might have landed on the water and drifted out with the tide.

Rudy Gaier, a young mechanic's assistant who had been a trapper in the area, accompanied Crosson as the two covered a large area around the inlet and extended their search north of Anchorage to Susitna Station. They communicated with the ground by dropping notes attached to small parachutes.

Crosson also flew Thyra Merrill and Cope west in the Waco to scan Merrill Pass and then, on a hunch, to Rainy Pass, where the Stillman-Durrell hunting party was still in the field. No, they had not seen Merrill's plane since he had dropped them at the camp a month before. Crosson and his searchers returned to Anchorage by way of the Skwentna River, flying over the inlet in total darkness.

During the next stage of the search, Crosson—with Thyra, Barnhill, and Gaier as observers—flew the New Standard down the west coast of the inlet, dropping notes to trappers. On September 26, they dropped two messages at Tyonek, less than fifty miles southwest of Anchorage across Cook Inlet.

NO ONE FELT A SENSE OF PANIC. BASED ON MERRILL'S SURVIVAL RECORD, EVERYONE ASSUMED HE HAD LANDED SOMEWHERE TO MAKE MINOR REPAIRS OR THAT BAD WEATHER HAD FORCED HIM OFF COURSE.

The first message landed near the native school and got no response. The second fell at the lower end of the village and brought a great deal of activity on the ground.

Finally two men spread pieces of canvas out along the beach. In large letters, they spelled out: 4 M DRIFT TIDE. The fliers interpreted the message to mean that the villagers had seen what could have been an airplane drifting four miles out into the inlet on the ebb tide. But flights had passed overhead without spotting either plane or wreckage.

Russel Merrill's sons Bob and Dick are pictured in front of *Anchorage No. 2* at Anchorage shortly after Bob's fifth birthday. Dick was six at the time.

Rudy Gaier took a boat down to Tyonek the same day to investigate. He discovered nothing and concluded that the natives had merely seen some natural debris. The U.S. marshal at Kenai, however, confirmed to Crosson and his searchers that a storm that hit on the 16th, about seven hours after Merrill flew off from Anchorage, had indeed swept up the east coast of the inlet as well as the west side, where Tyonek is situated.

Eielson flew once more through Merrill Pass, circling this time over George Shaben's cabin. Of course the deaf trapper might not have noticed

This map from the 1920s, indicating the area covered in the search for Russel Merrill after he disappeared on a flight from Anchorage on September 16, 1929, includes some handwritten notations by searches.

Merrill's plane even if it had passed over. It took three messages before Shaben understood what he was being asked. He consulted his diary to be sure what had happened on the 16th; he had not seen the plane.

Crosson tried the Kuskokwim once more on the outside chance that Merrill had taken a new course and arrived at Nyac without anyone seeing his plane along the way. Merrill had gasoline cached at various sites in the Mount Spurr region, and Crosson thought he might have detoured to one that was unknown to other pilots. Finding no news at Nyac, Crosson returned by a shortcut along the Stony River through a region inhabited almost entirely by natives. They kept records of passing planes, including notes on whether they were on pontoons, wheels, or skis. But their records revealed nothing.

By now the search had covered more than 10,000 miles. The focus of the search shifted south to Seward. Had Merrill continued south in hopes of avoiding the storm, or turned east to skirt it? A Captain Emswiler of the motor ship *Chase* said he had seen rockets fired off Cape Resurrection, just south of Seward. Had Merrill carried the signaling pistol the Aeronautics Branch had suggested? Captain Emswiler and his crew had searched off the cape without discovering the source of the rockets. A general alert was issued to mariners; the S.S. *Yukon* agreed to search the coastline on its way south to Seward, and the U.S. Coast Guard cutter *Unalga* was requested to search Resurrection Bay.

The search became even more intensive. Crosson, with Cope and Gaier as spotters, flew for six hours down Kamishak Bay on the west coast of Cook Inlet, near its southern end. It was hazardous flying because *Anchorage No. 2* was now on wheels, and the lower inlet had few places for a wheeled landing. They looked at anything floating in the water, overlooking nothing that might have a bearing on Merrill's disappearance. Coming up empty-handed, they returned to Anchorage.

Finally, after the search had crisscrossed Southcentral Alaska many times, the big break occurred agonizingly close to home. Nearly five weeks after Merrill disappeared, a man brought in a piece of airplane fabric that had washed up on the beach at Tyonek.

All along, Tyonek had been the most likely place for a clue to appear. People involved in the search had puzzled over the 4 M DRIFT TIDE message seen September 26 and had dispatched Rudy Gaier and the boat from Anchorage that same day. Although Gaier failed to find anything, pilots

FINALLY, AFTER THE SEARCH HAD CRISSCROSSED SOUTH-CENTRAL ALASKA MANY TIMES, THE BIG BREAK OCCURRED AGONIZINGLY CLOSE TO HOME.

People gather for dedication ceremonies September 25, 1932, for the Russel Hyde Merrill Memorial Beacon at Merrill Field Airport in Anchorage. The twenty-four-inch, high-intensity light atop the tower was the first aviation beacon in the Territory of Alaska.

combed the area from the air time after time.

The man who could have brought the search to an end was off by himself on a hunting trip, cut off from communication. Frank Smith, a native who owned a fish trap in the vicinity of Tyonek, had found the piece of fabric October 3. Unaware that a plane was missing, he left on a hunting trip without reporting his discovery. When he returned October 20, he showed the patch of fabric to the Tyonek school-teacher, William K. Leise, who immediately brought him to Anchorage.

Cope identified the fabric as a piece from the left horizontal stabilizer of *Anchorage No. 1*, Merrill's airplane. Cope had added that particular piece to the plane during its overhaul a year before, and he recognized his own work by the way the fabric was stitched. Moreover, no other plane in Alaska was painted the same sage-green color seen on the fabric. Cope had repainted the plane only a week before it was lost. The piece of fabric, measuring twelve by forty inches, was ragged on three sides and cleanly cut along the other. There was some thought that Merrill might have cut the fabric from the plane's tail with his knife in an attempt to make a sail.

The next day Barnhill and Cope flew to Tyonek to question the residents. The schoolteacher's wife said she had seen something out on the water the morning of September 17 but thought it was natural debris. Some of the natives had watched the object through field glasses until it disappeared. Now, with Barnhill's plane handy on the beach for comparison, they agreed that what they had seen could have been an airplane. It was a case of not seeing what they weren't looking for. They had not known then that an airplane was missing, so they had thought no more about it.

The search continued for another week, but was finally called off at the end of October. Every mile of territory where there was the faintest possibility of finding Merrill had been covered, most of it a number of times. Nothing more could be done. It was concluded that Merrill had experienced trouble

At dedication ceremonies for the Russel Hyde Merrill Memorial Beacon, the Rev. E. L. Winterberger described Merrill as "one of the early pioneers of aviation in Alaska who gave his best and his all in that work."

This bronze plaque honoring Russel Merrill was first placed in 1930 at the base of the new aviation beacon tower at Merrill Field. The plaque is now mounted on the control tower at the field, one of the busiest private airfields in the world.

with the plane, had been forced down on Cook Inlet, and was unable to make it to shore. He was never found.

In 1930 the Anchorage Women's Club launched a drive to construct a permanent memorial to Russel Merrill in the form of a tower and light beacon to aid landing at the new airfield. That summer, Anchorage Municipal Airport was renamed Merrill Field Airport.

The new forty-six-foot steel tower at Merrill Field, topped by a large high-intensity light, was turned over to the city on Sunday, September 25, 1932. The beacon in his memory meant that Merrill would continue to light the way for aviation in Alaska as he had done since 1925. A bronze plaque that was mounted at the base of this first aviation beacon in the Territory pictures Merrill in the cockpit of *Anchorage No. 1* and is inscribed:

TO THAT DAUNTLESS
PIONEER OF THE AIR
RUSSEL HYDE MERRILL
WHOSE LIFE'S AIM WAS
THE DEVELOPMENT OF
AVIATION IN ALASKA
SEPTEMBER 16, 1929

Soon after my father's death, my mother became determined to write the story of his life. Taking me and my brother, Dick, she moved from Anchorage to Portland, Oregon, in December 1929 and spent that winter writing the manuscript. It was never published, but it became an important basis for this present volume on the life of Russel Merrill.

In the spring of 1930, we moved to Palo Alto, California, where my mother took up flying. She organized the first women's flying club in the United States and became hostess of the new Curtiss-Wright flying field at San Mateo, California. On October 30, 1930, she earned the nineteenth women's commercial pilot's license issued in the United States.

Early in 1933, our little family moved up to Juneau, Alaska, where my mother bought a Lockheed Vega along with two Alaska pilots. They planned to start a flying business, but it didn't work out. Thyra met mining engineer Duncan MacLean in

Thyra Merrill became active as a flyer in California in the early 1930s. This photo was taken in 1930. She earned her U.S. commercial pilot's license on October 30, 1930, becoming only the nineteenth woman to do so.

Thyra Merrill MacLean joins sons Dick (left) and Bob in this 1944 photo. Dick served in the Army field artillery in World War II; Bob was a naval aviator.

Juneau, and they were married in October 1934. We moved to Seattle, where she became involved with family activities and raising me and Dick. She gave up flying.

Dick eventually worked as a physical therapist for the Veterans Hospital in Sacramento, California. He died of cancer in 1982, leaving his wife and three daughters.

I became a naval aviator in World War II and later owned and operated a sailmaking firm until my retirement in 1994. My wife, Margery, and I have four daughters.

My mother passed away November 27, 1984, at 82 years of age after a full and eventful life.

Robert Merrill MacLean

ROBERT MERRILL MACLEAN, son of Thyra and Russel Merrill, retired in 1994 from the sailmaking business he began as an outgrowth of his involvement in sailboat racing. He was a naval aviator in World War II, earned a degree in industrial engineering at the University of Washington, and later worked as a manager for Todd Shipyards in Seattle. He and his wife, Margery, parents of four daughters, live in Bellevue, Washington.

SEAN ROSSITER is the author of four books, including *Legends of the Air* (1990), which details the development and use of aircraft at Seattle's Museum of Flight. He is working on a biography of Father David Bauer, founder of Canada's national hockey team, and on a book about the de Havilland Beaver bush plane. He and his wife, Terri Wershler, live in Vancouver, B.C.